Qi Gong
for Total Wellness

ALSO BY DR. BAOLIN WU

Lighting the Eye of the Dragon: Inner Secrets of Taoist Feng Shui

(with Jessica Eckstein)

Qi Gong
for Total Wellness

Increase Your Energy, Vitality, and Longevity with the Ancient 9 Palaces System from the White Cloud Monastery

Dr. Baolin Wu

AND JESSICA ECKSTEIN

ILLUSTRATIONS BY OLIVER BENSON

 ST. MARTIN'S GRIFFIN ⚑ NEW YORK

www.stmartins.com

Book Design by Richard Oriolo

Library of Congress Cataloging-in-Publication Data
Wu, Baolin, 1954–
   Qi Gong for total wellness : increase your energy, vitality, and longevity with the Ancient 9 Palaces system from the White Cloud Monastery / Baolin Wu and Jessica Eckstein.—1st ed.
       p. cm.
    Includes index.
    ISBN-13: 978-0-312-26233-4
    ISBN-10: 0-312-26233-7
    1. Qi gong—Health aspects. 2. Physical fitness. I. Eckstein, Jessica. II. Title.
RA781.8. W7 2006
613.7'1—dc22

2006042356

First Edition: September 2006

10 9 8 7 6 5 4 3 2 1

To my Teachers

CONTENTS

The Way

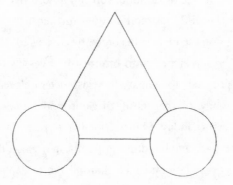

THE STANDARD-BEARER is Lao Zi. To speak of Qi Gong, of Taoism, of

Chinese thought and culture, one must return one's gaze to this lofty war-

den of ancient knowledge. His teachings were the culmination of thou-

sands of years of primordial shamanic insight and the foundation of all that

was yet to come. He left for the world the *Tao Te Ching*. This massive

accomplishment alone generated the first formal school of religion and philosophy in China. From his torch passed a fire that illuminated the mysticism of Zhuang Zi and the ethics of Confucius, and between these two mighty pillars, the poles of Chinese culture found their balance. To this day, all religious and political developments in China have had to answer to the influence of the Taoist worldview. The existence of Chinese civilization cannot be separated from the merit of Lao Zi, the father of Taoism and master of the Tao.

With the *Tao Te Ching*, Lao Zi provides a complete description of the journey toward oneness with the universe. But how to put one's feet to this path? On Zhongnan Mountain, at the spot where Lao Zi is said to have given his great lectures, rest two small stelae thought to date from the Han Dynasty. The characters of the *Tao Te Ching* are carved on one. On the other is carved Lao Zi's second great gift to humanity—the original thirteen movements of the 9 Palaces Solar Qi Gong. The *Tao Te Ching* and the 9 Palaces are inseparable. One provides the vision and the other the means to achieving it.

Through the practice of Qi Gong, you can absorb five thousand years of spiritual history. The Qi Gong tradition goes further back than this, into the prehistory of the Chinese people. Recorded references to Qi Gong cultivation date back 3,500 years, etched onto bronze ritual vessels from tombs excavated in Hunan province. They relate the existence of eleven energetic channels within the body. In this sense, Qi Gong and Chinese medicine share a common ancestry. Today Chinese medicine refers to fourteen main acupuncture meridians and hundreds of points. In a sense, the archaic eleven channels have a greater significance than all the research into points and meridians that came after, for they are the pathways of Qi flowing through the body that were most apparent to ancient people. If they felt a pain while toiling in the fields, they would observe how it spread through the body. A cure was understood as the method that would effectively stop and reroute this flow. Later, through trial and error, more was learned about controlling the flow by pressing points all over the body. Finding the control points came second. What came first was an understanding of the flow. Qi Gong is the study of this flow.

As a young neurophysiologist, Dr. Wu was sent to Kyoto University as part of a joint Chinese-Japanese research team, put together to chart the human nervous system in an attempt to pinpoint the physical locations of the acupuncture points. However, their research proved inconclusive. Even if you dissect every nerve and tissue in the body, you won't find the channels and meridians. Where are they? All there is is the Qi, the way Qi travels inside your body. All the terminology of meridians, channels, and points was developed to explain the pathways of Qi.

Qi Gong originated with the Taoists. There is no mention of Qi Gong in the earliest Buddhist sutras. From Lao Zi to Zhuang Zi, the preserver, and Confucius, the developer, the traditions of Taoism were built and expanded upon from generation to generation, branching and blending with Buddhist thought, practical alchemy, tribal forms of animism, and medical technique. Throughout this winding development, the study and cultivation of Qi was always held sacred and essential, and the Taoist Immortals and Masters were revered as its guardians.

What we know today as 9 Palaces Solar Qi Gong comes passed down to us from the traditions of the Quan Zhen, or Complete Reality School of Taoism. Founded by Wang Chongyang, whose life spanned the late Song and early Yuan dynasties, the Complete Reality School turned away from ceremonial and ritualistic forms of Taoist practice to focus instead on individual self-cultivation. Wang Chongyang saw that only Qi Gong practice had the power to unite the best aspects of Chinese thought—Confucian ethics, proto-Buddhist karmic cosmology and the dual foundations of the *Tao Te Ching* and the *I Ching*—within the heart, mind and body of the student. He completely reorganized the 9 Palaces exercises and wrote of and taught them extensively. Through his efforts, the heritage of the 9 Palaces Qi Gong has been passed down to this day. What we learn within these pages is the legacy of Wang Chongyang.

In his role as the originator of the Quan Zhen School, Wang Chongyang laid the foundation for the two greatest sanctuaries of Taoist scholarship in China, the White Cloud Monastery in Beijing and the Purple Cloud Monastery on Wu Dang Mountain. One is in the north, one is in the south, their influence encompassing all of Mainland China. From its earliest roots in the Tang Dynasty, the White Cloud Monastery grew to become the central repository of Taoist thought and study in the north, in large part due to the great fame and influence of Qiu Chuji, Wang's disciple and founder of the Dragon Gate Sect. The story of how the 9 Palaces came to the White Cloud Monastery, faded, and eventually bloomed anew begins with this relationship between master and student and leads to the present and the reason for this book. In recounting this history, held in silence behind the walls of the monastery, we create a new current in the motion of the Tao.

From Wang Chongyang and his seven disciples onward, it was decided that in each generation, the complete teachings would be passed to seven primary students: seven students per generation only, generation after generation. Despite the thousands of other students who played a part in the life of the White Cloud Monastery, there were always seven principal students. Of all the rules and regulations of monastic life, the primary policy was secrecy, especially in what was passed to the main disciples. What each student was taught was confidential and could never be shared with the outside world. There was a certain rationale behind this concealment. A teacher had a responsibility to really know and understand each student. If teachers didn't develop an individual relationship with their students and impersonally taught all comers, the wrong person might be taught and then could use what was learned for the wrong purpose. Beyond that, it was a question of aptitude. Not every student had the capability of mastering all that could be taught. So for Wang Chongyang and generations on, seven students were selected to become the inheritors of the undivided knowledge of their Taoist ancestors.

Wang Chongyang can be considered the spiritual ancestor of the White Cloud Monastery in that he unified all the theories and practices that became Complete Reality Taoism and 9 Palaces Qi Gong. However, he spent the last years of his life teaching and practicing the 9 Palaces in the south, at Wu Dang Mountain. Although Wang Chongyang's Complete Reality principles pervaded the scholarly culture at the White Cloud Monastery at its basic foundation, it was Qiu Chuji who built upon this foundation, establishing the White Cloud Monastery as the northern seat of the Complete Reality School and his own Dragon Gate Sect. While the White Cloud Monastery flourished as the wellspring of Taoist scholasticism, after the centuries of war and turmoil that was dynastic China, we cannot locate the original writings of Wang Chongyang's Wu Dang lectures.

Wang Chongyang lived to the age of 135, his entire life spent in the solar Yang practice of 9 Palaces Qi Gong. In spite of this, his disciple Qiu Chuji studied and practiced the Yin Gong of the 5 Centers Facing the Moon. Why did the student spend a lifetime in Yin practice when the master devoted his own exclusively to Yang? The answer is a story that is part of the secret oral tradition of the White Cloud Monastery, a story that is never told openly. Wang Chongyang did teach Qiu Chuji the 9 Palaces, but instead of profiting from his practice, his body violently reacted against the Yang energy he was taking in and he began to hemorrhage and vomit blood. He survived his ordeal, but was enjoined by Wang Chongyang to stop studying 9 Palaces, and only practice 5 Centers Facing the Moon from then on. Master Wang told him, "Your body is unsuitable for the 9 Palaces. By developing yourself with the 5 Centers, you will be able to focus like no other on the energies of the I Ching and from that, become a great master of Feng Shui. In this way, you will use the forces of the unknown to find your fortune and further the teachings of Taoism."

Qiu Chuji heeded his master's admonition and spent years living deep within the Dragon Gate Cave, refining his occult abilities. He eventually rose to great fame as an advisor to emperors and warlords, including Genghis Khan. His abilities as a seer and oracle, as well as a military advisor using Feng Shui to position the troops on the fields of battle, earned him the necessary support to promote Complete Reality Taoism and erect many temples and monasteries. His wide following established the White Cloud Monastery as the central headquarters for Taoist learning that it is still known even today.

Since Qiu Chuji's reputation was built on his peerless mastery of 5 Centers Qi Gong, all his students in the White Cloud Monastery dedicated a large portion of their studies to it. Yet toward the end of his life, he advocated a renewed emphasis on the 9 Palaces. Qiu felt it was strictly his own mistake that he had learned the practice incorrectly from his teacher. He regretted that his students would not experience its great benefits because of his error and did what he could to pass down what he knew as part of his

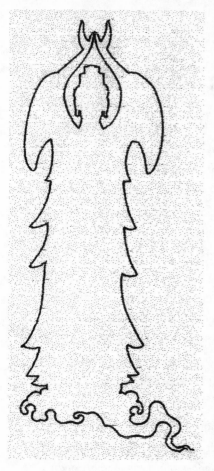

tradition. However, the lineage of 9 Palaces Qi Gong study at the White Cloud Monastery was weakened enough that by the end of the Qing Dynasty, hardly a soul there knew anything about it.

Between 1927 and 1934, the White Cloud Monastery issued a formal invitation to the monks of the Purple Cloud Monastery at Wu Dang Mountain to send an emissary to come teach the 9 Palaces again in the north.

With great ceremony, the Purple Cloud leaders called for a convocation of all the monks of the monastery. Of the 705 monks who gathered, one would have to be selected. The first priority was that he be one of the direct inheritors of the 9 Palaces, whose lineage could be traced back through the generations to the original teachings of Wang Chongyang. Second, he must be a meritorious individual, respected by all. Third, his scholarship must be impeccable, having complete knowledge of the books, sacred texts, and practical arts of Taoism. A single person who could best embody the solid foundation of the southern school would be required to rebuild from the ground up the foundation of the north.

After seven days of heavy testing, a worthy representative was selected. Not only was he chosen as one of the original lineage inheritors of the 9 Palaces, he was also picked for his position as the top martial artist in the country. There were others with names more famous than his, but all respected the authority as well as the erudition of this unusual man, who would be sent to the north to rebuild the tradition of the 9 Palaces and to eventually become Dr. Wu's guardian and teacher. And thus, after centuries, was the original knowledge of Wang Chongyang returned to its northern birthplace. It is in his honor, as in honor of Lao himself, that this book is presented.

Du Xinlin, known as the Master of the Purple Luminescence, was an extraordinary modern seer. From his earliest childhood to his mystical passing from this plane, he lived his life as something more than a mere man. Tales of his feats of divination, martial artistry, and healing are recorded within the annals of both the Purple Cloud and White Cloud Monasteries. In fact, his earliest beginnings earmarked his special fate.

He was an orphaned child, abandoned to the swelling waters when the river flooded his village. Amazingly, he survived the flood completely alone. He recalled being protected in the wild by a tiger and weaned on her milk. Later, at age four, he was found by a wandering Taoist hermit who raised him in the wilderness of Wu Dang Mountain, and eventually brought him to the monastery. All his life, he lived and learned with animals. He kept vultures as his pets, along with a tiger and a crane. His martial arts were not learned from traditional teachers. He played with his pets and gained his martial arts prowess from them. Dr. Wu has an early childhood memory of seeing his master pick up a massive tree trunk and fling it down with no effort. He would toss a heavy traditional clothes-washing roller for his daily practice. He slept balanced on a rope hung between two trees. He would eat fruits and vegetables by biting them while they still hung on branch or vine. Whenever he traveled or gave a public speech, vultures and eagles would fly alongside him. Dr. Wu remembers being amazed at the quantities of unusual birds following above him at all times. There is no way to describe a man like Du Xinlin from a contemporary perspective. The words aren't there, but the memories and stories linger on.

In the 1930s Master Du came to Beijing, arriving at the White Cloud Monastery, where he began teaching the 9 Palaces. It was not taught to outsiders, kept within the circle of the monastery. All his life, Master Du kept back from the daily press of the public, only agreeing to help the very sick and desperate who came within the confines of the monastery seeking succor. Occasionally he would travel quietly to pay respects and make offerings at shrines and temples across China, in later years accompanied by the young Dr. Wu. His great love, though, was to stay inside the walls of the White Cloud Monastery, tending to his animals or strolling in the fields and fruit orchards that provided their bounty to the monks.

According to Dr. Wu's other teachers, Master Du's martial arts were more advanced than even Qiu Chuji's and Wang Chongyang's. Many came to challenge him, but no one could best him. He could hold off his opponents just by raising his sleeve. With that one gesture, his internal force was so obvious that his would-be challengers would concede before the fight even began. Despite his life of seclusion, he was involved in training many better-known martial artists of the time. These stories were kept as secrets by the Taoist brothers, but it serves to honor the abilities of this remarkable man and the power of 9 Palaces Qi Gong to relate a few of them here.

Master Du's most famous martial arts student is a name that has gone down in the annals of modern martial arts history. Wang Xiangzhai is recognized around the world as the great twentieth-century popularizer of Chinese martial arts inside and outside China. As an unbeatable master, he traveled extensively, taught, wrote, and established a number of forums and organizations for the study and dissemination of scientific martial arts. There are many stories of the Chinese, Japanese, and Western fighters who came from all around to be bested by his superior skills.

All his life, he practiced the 9 Palaces. With his lifetime of study and his public persona, he did more than any other figure to publicize the energetic principles of the 9 Palaces. His books and lectures are famed for discussing the body's natural "springing power." The body can express energy like the release of a coiled spring. Wang would often compare the strength of this force to the power unleashed by a person maddened with anger or distress. Even ten men can't hold down a man or woman overtaken by his or her own primal intensity. Wang's writings go to great lengths to conceptualize the body as a spring and the personal aspects involved in allowing force to come out naturally from inside. However, he refrained from directly discussing the full scope of this force. In fact, it is the energy of the 9 Palaces.

The coiled, springlike aspect of natural force is only the most basic element of a complex process. Practicing 9 Palaces Qi Gong develops this force not as an end in and of itself, but as a means of igniting an electrifying energy. Once you can call forth this bioelectrical power, everything that comes at you can be repelled. Just a touch can stun with the impact of an electric shock. This is how Wang, like his master before him, was so successful. Master Du recognized Wang's natural abilities and leadership skills and trained him in order to send him out as a living demonstration of the power of Qi Gong, expressed through martial arts. Practice Qi Gong, and anything that hits you will spring off. However, with its protective and propulsive qualities, this same force can equally be used for healing work or taken further into higher levels of spiritual development. It comes from a unified effort of body, mind, and spirit. It cannot be grasped on a purely intellectual level. It must be practiced to be understood. To understand it is to understand yourself. With this under-standing comes a passage into a new realm of energy and awareness.

The dramatic tales of his students' accomplishments pale in comparison to Master Du's own, less public, story. After drawing a certain amount of attention to the White Cloud Monastery and, despite his efforts, to himself personally, his reputation reached the attention of Mao Zedong, who was still struggling to consolidate his power at the time. Approached by the Great Leader three times, Master Du retreated to a cave outside Beijing, refusing to see him for any reason. At last, the Taoist Brothers begged their teacher to return to the monastery and meet with Mao just once, worried that he was too powerful a figure to deny.

On the day of his audience, the master came forth from his quarters. Mao saluted him with the traditional prayerful postures, but Master Du cut him short, telling him he could not accept any of his respect. He made Mao lie down on a large flat rock to settle his Qi and tersely asked for his ques-tions. Mao had two questions: how long would he be in power and how long would he live. Immediately Master Du answered, "Eighty-three. Forty-one," turned around, and left. Mao was so struck by his encounter with the Master that for the rest of his life he used the characters for forty-one and eighty-three as his personal inscription. As it came to pass, he did indeed live into his eighty-third year and held power as the chairman of the Communist Party from 1935 until his passing in 1976. This did not prevent the oppression of monks and nuns, the banning of traditional Taoist practices, and the even-tual seizure of the White Cloud Monastery's assets during the worst days of the Cultural Revolution.

After his meeting with Mao, Master Du kept more and more to himself, staying within his own quarters and rarely receiving visitors. When Dr. Wu was brought to the White Cloud Monastery as a four-year-old boy dying of leukemia, Master Du quickly took him under his protection, becoming his guardian and directing his treatment. After a year, he was completely cured and became the Master's student and attendant. Before dawn, he would wake with the other monks, recite the Sutras, and practice Qi Gong. Then he would leave the monastery to go to school, returning in the afternoon for martial arts training, religious studies, and assisting in the daily rituals and offerings.

Master Du also had special assignments for his young charge. Some were tedious, like the months spent standing on a street corner counting the people who passed by, or inexplicable, like the entire summer spent reading a book with blank pages. Sometimes he just followed his teacher in the fields, asking the unruly questions of a bored child. If he got an answer at all, it was always something he could learn from. In his old age, Master Du made a final trip across the country to Tibet, to the Potala Palace, with a group of his students, including young Wu. In their travels, the Qi of every cloud, every land formation, and every river and stream was discussed. In his final years, the master left Beijing for West Mountain, in Yunnan Province. He said the White Cloud Monastery was too noisy and the Qi overhead was disrupted by too many airplanes. It was true that history was spinning faster and faster. Communist China was in the throes of the Cultural Revolution and the traditions of practicing Taoists, as well as their personal safety, were endangered. For a time, Dr. Wu lived with his teacher there, but as a teenage boy from an intellectual and Westernized family, he eventually returned to the capital to prepare for his future studies at university.

At the age of 116, Master Du left the earthly plane. He lived his life as a towering mystic and master of the Taoist arts and had decided to dedicate his passing to a demonstration of the truth of his lifelong beliefs. What he accomplished was a manifestation of the power of Qi Gong few have ever attempted and no one had ever truly succeeded at in the modern era. His accomplishment is a significant event in Chinese cultural history. To present the inner teachings of 9 Palaces Microcosmic Orbit Qi Gong is a testament to his attainment and the fulfillment of his last living wish.

A few years before, when Dr. Wu was still living with him, Master Du told him that he believed that Lao Zi, Wang Chongyang, and all his other teachers were waiting for him in the Nine Central Heavens. As Lao Zi's disciple, he was ready to join him there. He told the young boy about the Rainbow Body that a worthy believer could cultivate inside his mortal body and that if his righteousness merited it, it could leave the body with consciousness and spirit intact, instead of physical death, to fly up to Heaven in a rainbow of light.

Transubstantiation and eternal life that bypasses corporeal death has a long tradition in the East. It is known as *hong hua*, literally a form of the word "rainbow" that can be used as a noun or verb: The Rainbow Body is cultivated within a righteous person's physical body at the moment in passing. Taoist and Tibetan Buddhist tradition is peppered with stories of famous monks, hermits, and high lamas who attempted this feat by devoting their lives to meditation, training, and saintly acts. The ones who attained the Rainbow Body were revered forever as saints and Immortals. Those who tried to pass over by "rainbow-ing" but did not succeed in leaving the world without a trace of their physical remains left behind were still venerated, the remnants of their bodies kept enshrined as holy relics. One such relic had been housed in the White Cloud Monastery when Dr. Wu was a boy there. It looked like a tiny, shriveled little man about a foot and a half high, covered in leathery, age-darkened skin. It was explained to him that if there were any portions of the Rainbow Body practitioner's body that had not been properly purified before his or her attempt, it would be left behind in a shrunken, desiccated form.

Master Du told young Wu the day and the hour he was going to Rainbow and made him swear to be there to watch his attempt, no matter what. Soon he became so focused on his future that he would spend the whole day quietly whispering, "I'm going, I'm going" to himself. In the beginning, the boy thought, "My teacher must be too old . . . what is he talking about, all day long just saying, 'I'm going, I'm going!' Toward the end, when he had to return to Beijing for his studies, he remembers pleading with his master to stop worrying and continuously talking about it with him, assuring him that he would skip school and do whatever else he had to do to be there and watch him when he was ready to leave. Even with his childhood of Taoist training, the teenage Dr. Wu was still skeptical of his master's unconventional ways and crazy ideas. But when that particular day finally came to pass, Master Du attained his Rainbow Body. Ever since, Dr. Wu deeply believes.

The day before he was set to make his attempt, Master Du called his young student to his side. He told him, "Tomorrow I will be rainbowed. I am going to my place in the Ninth Level of Heaven to do my practice there. I am going to continue my studies with my master Lao Zi and sit at his feet, learning what he teaches, but from now on you are going to have to study by yourself. You're going to have to work hard. Of all my students, you have learned much, but I am worried for you. You don't study hard, you are skeptical in your practice, and yet you absorb my teachings so well. All that I know, I must pass to you because none of my other students have the wisdom and insight that you barely realize that you possess. Because of the troubles in China, there is no time or place to find someone better than you to pass these traditions to."

As he sat in a tub of hot water strewn with fragrant flower petals, being washed by his student, he talked to him at length about the key points of 9 Palaces and 5 Centers Qi Gong. He told him of the real meaning of martial arts. When you learn martial arts, you are not going after specific movements, or their proper visual form, or if your hand moves correctly or not. You have to have the feel of a natural force living within you. If you feel it rising inside you, then you can bring it out with power and dynamism. Why does it take more than one person to catch, control, and subdue an insane person? They have left behind all the things that have separated them from their original abilities. Within your own original abilities lies your power. Why was Wang Xiangzhai so successful in his martial arts? Because he was able to bring out his own personal essence, his own unique force. There are special trainings to accomplish this. If you just focus on supple movements it might be good exercise, but if you really want to learn true striking power, true healing power, true energetic power, the basic foundation is Qi Gong.

They talked together like that all night, the student bathing the master, the master transmitting his last words of wisdom, from eight o'clock in the evening to five the next morning. When Master Du had said all that he could, he faced his apprentice seriously. "I know you question what I have taught you, but tomorrow I will show you the reality of this knowledge. Of all my students, you are the one with the most doubts. You have difficulty trusting in me or believing in the teachings. But I believe, because I believe my own eyes. I believe in myself. I know you are a good student. You're a very smart person. You have good comprehension and understanding, you can see things through, clearly and quickly. You have your own measure of wisdom. If tomorrow I fail to attain the Rainbow Body, all I ask is that you bury my remains in the place I have directed you. You can go on with your life and never think about Taoism again. I have high hopes that if tomorrow you see with your own two eyes that I have indeed succeeded, you will vow to teach the 9 Palaces nine hundred and ninety nine times in honor of the truth you have been witness to."

That day, the temple was decorated with flowers and auspicious banners. Monks with musical instruments played continuously. Over one hundred people were assembled, including silent monitors from the Communist Party. Master Du sat in complete stillness and silence on a silken meditation cushion embroidered with dragons. At high noon, the moment for the transition had arrived. At first he remained immobile. At his side, Dr. Wu momentarily grasped his shoulder with a small shake. Suddenly his teacher flared with a burst of energy. Still enclosed in profound contemplation, his body began to levitate, spinning straight up from its cushion, rising by itself and revolving faster and faster. Turning so fast his body was a blur, he hovered for a fleeting moment just above the heads of the stunned onlookers. The solidity of his form shifted, became indistinct. His outline evaporated into red smoke; a piercing ray of red light shot straight through the center of the sun, transfixing him; and at once, the Master was gone. He had departed. No trace was left, except a pleasing fragrance that filled the courtyard for hours after.

How can this be understood? How can it be explained? For the rest of the afternoon, Dr. Wu and his companions were lost in wonder and shocked speechlessness. They had been witness to proof of the heights a lifetime's study in Qi Gong could achieve. True evidence of perfected attainment,

Master Du's final act on this plane was a testament to the reality of the potent forces unleashed by the 9 Palaces. Ever since then, Dr. Wu deeply and beyond doubt believes in its power.

The Rainbow Body is an enormous question mark for science. What is the nature of this transformation? How did the Master go? Where is he now? So far, no one knows. No amount of analysis can penetrate this mystery. However we might like a scientific explanation of this phenomenon, the tools have yet to be developed that could begin to measure it. Even as a medical doctor and a research scientist with a background in neurophysiology, Dr. Wu feels that currently there still is little likelihood of creating an effective methodology for its study. Years before attaining the Rainbow Body, Master Du told his student the day and hour he would be taking his leave. Dr. Wu was a skeptical young man more influenced by his Western studies than by his elderly guardian. When it actually came to pass, Dr. Wu could not deny what he had seen with his own eyes.

Witnessing his master's transubstantiation shook his most basic assumptions of reality to such a degree that he was literally struck speechless. For more than two hours, he was unable to utter even a single word. Master Du was there one moment and the next he was gone. He vanished in a puff of smoke, just like in a fairy story. Afterward, Dr. Wu kept thinking back and realized that he had already been shown proof of his master's unexplainable capabilities. A month before his Rainbow passage, his Taoist brothers asked him to take a picture with them. Master Du had always refused to allow his picture to be taken. He did not want to be exposed to the camera's flash. Because they knew how much he loved his youngest student, they sent Dr. Wu to coax him into joining a group photo. Because of the wild vultures that Master Du kept untethered within his quarters, no one could even get near enough to him to pull him over for a quick photo other than the young Wu, whom the birds recognized from his years of living at his master's side. Thanks to the teenager's efforts, the brothers got their picture surrounding their revered teacher. Strangely, when the picture was developed, Master Du's image was gone. Everybody else was standing just as they had been photographed. But his spot was empty, just a faint blurry smudge. The Master had already reached the level of his Rainbow Body with his practice. His body was already invisible, his physical matter clear like a crystal.

Throughout the generations, there have been many nameless Taoists who have accomplished remarkable feats as a result of their sincere cultivation. Unlike other religions that encourage more public veneration of their saints and holy people, from early on the Taoists refrained from open demonstrations of their abilities. Even the basic philosophical teachings of Taoism were not widely disseminated to the public. Rather, they were held within the ranks of masters and students, layer within layer of inner circles. The traditions of secrecy and oral instruction in part developed due to the personal nature of one's studies. Qi Gong is a self-regulating discipline, bringing to the practitioner only what he is capable of achieving. The actual practices are simple and few, although there is a wide range of individual experiences.

A Taoist who practiced for a lifetime without discovering a new general theory or technique that could be universally applied would see no reason to discuss or write of his or her personal experiences. It would be considered improper to do anything more than work hard on developing your own unique abilities until your cultivation brought you to a level of impersonal realization and objective truth that could truly be beneficial for others' personal growth. Also, Taoist masters would not teach you anything they had not first tested themselves. It is a point of honor to only present information that has been personally experienced and proven, out of respect for their own teachers and to preserve their own moral and ethical cultivation. This is why the most significant Taoist texts often focus on simple but broad concepts and practical knowledge. It's not that the esoteric meanings of these teachings were covered up or watered down for public consumption. Rather, Taoism's insistence on personal responsibility in one's spiritual studies spotlights the importance of finding your own path from truism to the deeper understanding of fundamental truth. The theories and procedures of 9 Palaces Microcosmic Orbit Qi Gong presented here have all been proven through the efforts of the ancestors of its lineage and practiced at great length by Dr. Wu and his patients and students. However, 9 Palaces Qi Gong is something you cultivate inside yourself. You can't buy it with money, and the most revered master can only point you in the right direction. It's your own self-discipline, your own personal efforts, that will lead to understanding and accomplishment.

There are unknowable aspects of 9 Palaces Qi Gong that can only be grasped from within one's own practice. The remarkable achievements of towering figures such as Master Du Xinlin are presented as a source of inspiration to motivate you in your studies. We want you to believe in this practice and want you to learn it as thoroughly as possible. As long as you practice with sincerity, it will bring you good results, some simple and obvious, some that cannot be imagined until you experience them for yourself. Not only can it help you build better health, it can also change and awaken processes and energies inside your body that you never knew you would be capable of.

To simplify, first and foremost, 9 Palaces Qi Gong training is for longevity. This is the basic, immediate benefit when you practice 9 Palaces. Second, 9 Palaces is for changing your fate. Certain aspects of our lives are predetermined: which family we are born into, our gender. Marriage, knowledge, problems, and obstacles all share special relationships with our destiny. Our abilities are no less than the president's. Why, then, is he president and we aren't? How can we change this prearrangement in our lives? When is it better to just go with the flow and accept our fates? Sometimes humans can control a great river's levels, and sometimes Nature takes the reins despite our best efforts and causes flooding or drought. The *I Ching* discusses how atmospheric changes alter the prearranged destinies of the Earth and its inhabitants. Lao Zi studied the physical rhythms of these atmospheric shifts.

The 9 Palaces is the method for making these changes in your own environment and life.

The third purpose of 9 Palaces Qi Gong is for developing spiritual awareness. While it is not a religion, Qi Gong can heighten your personal connection to your faith. For a Taoist, religion is only part of a larger array of communication with Nature, God, and Cosmos. As large as there is no limit, as small as there is no inside, within a single grain of sand, a universe exists. Yin and Yang are the back and front of the sun. Lao Zi's primary theories can be understood from exploring the Qi that fills every aspect of existence. Realization comes from cultivating and refining the body's natural forces. With 9 Palaces practice, you are planting a seed that will grow into a force for harmony, peace, and righteousness.

This book does not attempt to prove the existence of Qi, except by presenting an effective method for experiencing it within your own body. Don't take anything at face value. You must practice the 9 Palaces for yourself and make your own determinations. Each person has an individual connection to Qi within the confines of his or her unique physical, intellectual, and emotional perceptions and abilities. This is not an academic thesis on the history of Taoism. It is a record of the process that passes between a teacher and a student of Qi Gong. Information that ranges from simple health advice to profound occult secrets revealed is put forth equally, for the plain reason that they share the same source, the postures and exercises of the 9 Palaces Microcosmic Orbit Qi Gong. It is our deepest intention to discuss the full potential of this powerful form in a clear and useful manner, removed from secrecy and misdirection. In this way, we give honor to the heritage of Lao Zi; the saints, sages, and immortals who followed in his wake; and especially to the memory of Master Du Xinlin and the lineage of the Dragon Gate Sect. Use this book as a living tool to aid you along your own personal path and know that with your sincere participation, you too are a part of this tradition.

Groundwork

THE 9 PALACES

IF YOU HAVE ever touched down in a new city for the first time, as

you've gotten behind the wheel of your car, you may have wondered, how

am I going to reach my destination? The road map is filled with every kind of

street and highway, all leading in the same direction. The key is to find the

route that is the most direct. The same thing holds true for Qi Gong. How can the healing power of the Qi most effectively be brought into the body? In order to make contact with the energy of the universe, the most efficient pathways for communication must be opened. These are not secret channels unleashed by mysterious initiations. In fact, these pathways are already in place. We are born with them. The nine openings of the body—eyes, ears, nostrils, mouth, urethra, and anus—allow all of the messages from the world around us to come in. They are the 9 Palaces of the 9 Palaces Microcosmic Orbit Qi Gong.

Our sense organs are two-way communication devices. With our eyes, we look out on the world. At the same time, they reveal our every mood and desire; they are the "windows of the soul." With our mouths, we intake food and drink and express our thoughts and wishes. We inhale and exhale through the nose, and the same organs that are used for elimination are also used for sexual pleasure. As we will see, even our ears, which on the surface seem only to listen for sound, reveal truths about health and personality just as surely as the eyes.

The nine opening of the body are related to nine major internal organs. In Chinese medicine, the kidneys are associated with the ears. The urethra is connected to the bladder and uterus. The anus connects to the intestines, the mouth to the stomach and spleen. When you catch a cold, your nose and lungs both get congested. One of the first signs of hepatitis is a yellowing of the eyes, an obvious reflection of their connection to the liver. In order to stay healthy, the channels that run between the organs and senses must be kept clean, clear, and open.

From a Taoist perspective, the nine openings not only allow us to interact with the physical world, but are also our means of communication with the entire universe. Health and well-being arise from the free exchange of internal and external energy. Cleaning the 9 Palaces creates an open conduit for the circulation of Qi. Human life is a constant process of acting and reacting to the messages of Heaven and Earth. Finding the most natural way to do this unlocks the door to longevity and spiritual growth.

It has become increasingly more of a challenge to live a natural life. Precautions must be taken at every step to maintain one's health. Some ways are obvious. When it's cold and damp outside, bundle up to stay warm. When it's very hot, wear lighter clothes and cut down on physical exertion. Adjusting one's behavior to the changing seasons is a commonsense way to avoid getting sick, but other environmental influences are less apparent. Excess electromagnetic radiation, microwaves, pollution in the water and air, and pesticides in our food all put undue stress on our body systems.

Along with the environmental impact, there are other, more intangible circumstances that affect our health. Some illness originates in the organs, but today both Chinese and Western medicine recognize the important role that stress and emotional imbalance play in impacting physical health. For thousands of years, the Taoists have researched the connection between body and mind. In addition, their ancient wisdom has carefully observed and compiled data on the subtle interplay of cosmic forces that are beyond the scope of ordinary experience, yet nevertheless are at work with us at all times.

Based on their understanding of the medical, psychological, and spiritual processes of life, 9 Palaces Microcosmic Orbit Qi Gong has been handed down through the generations as a means of dealing with every level of influence the outer world exerts upon the human organism.

The 9 Palaces Qi Gong is a powerful practice that cleanses and balances the body through a combination of movement, visualization, and specialized breathing. Working with the energy of the sun, it trains the practitioner to expel toxins and intake healthy Qi through the pores and the nine openings of the body. The Qi is then guided through specific channels related to the organs in a sequence that amplifies its energy while strengthening the meridians and awakening circulation in the Microcosmic Orbit. The transformed Qi is then available to be brought into the body at a deep cellular level for healing or storage for future use. As we will explore throughout this book, these exercises provide both a complete cardiovascular workout and a powerful method of internal alchemy at one and the same time.

YOUR BODY IS A BATTERY

THE TENDENCY IN life is to be active, moving around, on the go. No matter how much or how little we do in a day, we are constantly expending the energy stored in our organs. It flows out through our senses as we strive to interact with our environment. There is nothing inherently wrong with this. It's a fact of life, whether you live in a village or in a big city. Of course, modern living's constant sensory overload doesn't help, but it's a mistake to think it was ever any easier in some glorified ancient past. Yin exists at all times within Yang. As the energy of life is used up, the forces of dissolution inevitably take over. Even if you spent the rest of your life sitting in a dark cave with your eyes closed, you would not be able to stop this process from happening. Logically, the only thing that is going to help is to make sure that you can at all times bring more living energy into your system than you give out.

One of the great goals of Taoist cultivation is to lead a long, healthy, and productive life, helping others to the best of one's abilities. The main objective of 9 Palaces Qi Gong is longevity. This is accomplished by maximizing the body's ability to absorb vital Yang energy from the sun. The sun is the source of all growth and life on the planet. Solar energy is the embodiment of Yang energy. In fact, the Chinese term for the sun is *tai yang*, or "great Yang." The light of the sun provides nourishment to everything it touches. The 9 Palaces Qi Gong opens the line of communication between you and the solar force, and by extension with the living energy of all things.

The sun is used to balance and strengthen the body's bioelectric system. All objects, both living and dead, are surrounded by an electromagnetic field. Matter is held together on a subatomic level by magnetism created by the oscillation of positive and negatively charged ions. In other words, our bodies are vibrating masses of electricity. The circuitry in the brain, the impulses of the nervous system, the movements of the muscles—all are governed by finely tuned currents of electricity. Recent research shows that mechanical objects emit forms of electromagnetic radiation that can be harmful to living organisms. Reports of cancer have been linked to the emissions from high-tension power lines, computer monitors, cellular phones, and so on. Some believe the sudden extreme spikes of energy that these items give off disrupt the electrical balance in the body, causing an increased likelihood of cell dysfunction and mutation. The use of 9 Palaces Qi Gong helps to protect against these toxic emissions by increasing the power of the body's own currents. The practice forms a protective sheath around our delicate cellular and neural circuitry, rather like a surge protector that safeguards a computer from shorting out during a thunderstorm.

This protective envelope of bioelectricity, built up by steady practice of the 9 Palaces, is of great benefit to the immune system for a number of reasons. Besides keeping negative radiation at bay, a stronger electrical system develops an increasing capacity to absorb more beneficial energy into the body. Basically, you are streamlining the electrically based systems in your body, such as the nervous system and brain, to work more efficiently and at higher levels of operation. By practicing 9 Palaces Qi Gong, you are turning your body into a giant, self-charging battery.

This works in a few ways at once. Going back to the concept of electromagnetic fields, the exercises of the 9 Palaces, and especially their order within the form, are designed to tune your own field more closely with those of the sun and the Earth. Vibrating together at the same frequency, your energies merge. Not only do you become more connected with the sun and the Earth, this process also allows for their energy to be fully assimilated into your body. This balances and invigorates the nervous system. Combined with specialized stretches that open up the meridian points along the length of the spine, nerve impulses then will be able to be sent unobstructed to all the organs of the body, greatly enhancing the body's healing capabilities.

The immune system is not only improved by increasing your nervous system's ability to regulate the body. The practice of 9 Palaces Qi Gong may seem like very still, quiet practice. Actually, it provides the body with a complete cardiovascular workout, by combining breathing with internal isometric exercise and visualization. In Chinese, the term for oxygen is *yang qi. Qi* is breath. By using controlled breathing to pack the rib cage and abdomen with air, you are massaging your internal organs with Qi. Pressurizing the torso from inside stretches and tones the fascia from the inside out. The 9 Palaces Qi Gong also trains the body to use the entire surface of the skin to breathe, which stimulates and detoxifies the organs and circulatory systems. Over time, not only will your body feel energized and rejuvenated, but you will also find that you have physically and mentally entered a deeper state of communication with the cosmos.

ENERGY CIRCULATION IN THE BODY

THE 9 PALACES Qi Gong involves a very sophisticated interaction with the flow of Qi as it moves around and within the body. Today, an awareness of Qi Gong has developed due to growing interest in Chinese medicine and acupuncture. It is assumed that knowledge of the acupuncture points and meridians are of primary importance to successfully treat patients. However, in ancient times the emphasis was quite the reverse. It was understood that all the acupuncture points could be forgotten, but the meridian channels would have to be remembered in order to recognize the manner in which Qi travels through the body. If you dissect a body, no matter how hard you look, you won't be able to find the meridians. The meridians are only one way of understanding the circulation of Qi.

Chinese medicine and Taoist healing do not always precisely line up. When practicing 9 Palaces Qi Gong, you move the Qi through pathways and stations that may seem similar to certain meridians or acupuncture points, but they are not the same in every case. You will find that you will be limiting yourself if you try to find a direct, one-to-one correlation between them all the time. As you practice Qi Gong, you are gradually turning your entire body into a pathway for the Qi. Why intake Qi through an acupuncture point if you can absorb through every pore in your body? Why fill a meridian with Qi if you can fill your whole arm (or leg, or torso) with it, from the outer surface of the skin to deep within the marrow and down into the cells?

In 9 Palaces Qi Gong, Qi is collected in the three *dan*. These are the main energy storage centers in the body—lower, middle, and upper. They can be found by forming your hands in the shape of an open triangle, with thumbs and forefingers touching. Place your hands over your lower abdomen with the tips of the thumbs meeting in the navel. The space inside the triangle is the exact size and location of your lower *dan*. The middle *dan* is found by turning your triangle right side up and holding it centered between the two nipples. The upper *dan* is also found with the upright triangle, placed with the thumbs right over the eyebrows.

The three *dan* are more commonly known as the three *dan tian* (often spelled *tien*), but this is not completely accurate. In the inner tradition of Qi Gong, only the lower *dan* is referred to as the *dan tian*. The character for *tian* represents a farmer's field. A field is a place where life grows. In a field, seeds can be sown, nurtured, and then harvested. Though the *dan* do not have exact reference points within the physical body, the lower *dan tian* and the womb are closely related. Whether you are male or female, your *dan tian* is your body's fertile pasture. Gathering Qi into the *dan tian* plants a seed of new energy inside oneself. Cultivating the energy of the *dan tian* causes this new energy to grow.

This conception and gestation period is not unlike a pregnancy. As the energy of the *dan tian* consolidates, it rises up through the body, passing through the middle and upper *dan*, and out through the top of the head.

Released, this new force allows one's spirit to achieve a greater alignment with the forces of Heaven and Earth. There are many obscure references to this work in the ancient Taoist alchemical texts. Cryptic allusions to "nurturing the Qi for nine months" and "the Immortal Fetus" simply are discussing this natural process that begins when we are born, but must be completed through practice and cultivation of the energy pathways of the body. The effort and attention paid to unblocking and nourishing the three *dan* is an outstanding characteristic of 9 Palaces Qi Gong.

Besides gathering in and storing energy, the three *dan* act as switching points that allow energy to be directed through many different channels. As we will see, there are many places in the 9 Palaces form where you will be asked to swallow air or saliva down to the *dan tian*, use the middle *dan* to send energy into the hands, and so on. As you begin practicing the form, you may use your breath and muscles to move Qi around, or you might find that visualizing the energy as it moves might work better for you. Do whatever feels most comfortable. Over time, you will find that you will be able to do both at once, and even begin to sense the Qi flowing through you in subtle ways that don't require visualization or attention to movement. This may be due to the fact that after a certain amount of practice, the nervous system's ability to sense the Qi has been enhanced. Though there may be no scientific explanation for this as yet, as you experience the flow of Qi through your body, you will know it to be true.

No matter how you perceive the circulation of Qi, there are certain basic channels that are unblocked when practicing 9 Palaces. First of all, there is the Microcosmic Orbit. Opening the pathway of the Microcosmic Orbit is so fundamental that our practice is often referred to as *9 Palaces Microcosmic Orbit Qi Gong*. Both the Yin and Yang channels are exercised in the practice of 9 Palaces Qi Gong. The positioning of Yin and Yang on the body is a complicated subject. The ancient *I Ching* scholar Bai Nan Zi discussed Yin and Yang as the difference between where the sun can and cannot reach. Where the sunlight shines brightest is Yang and where shadow prevails is Yin. Looking at the four directions, southern and eastern exposures receive the greatest amount of light, while northern and western exposures only gain the sunlight as it is waning from the sky. In the *I Ching*, the north symbolizes the human element. Therefore, man symbolically stands in the north, facing south toward the sun.

This philosophy has had a long history of influence on Chinese culture. Rituals and honors have always been bestowed facing south. In Taoist Feng Shui, the position of everything from your front door to your bed can be set toward the south, for gathering harmonious Qi. Even the queue, the famous haircut of the Qing Dynasty that signified allegiance to the emperor in the face of encroaching Western domination, typified this concept. The long ponytail at the back of the head, never to be cut, represented the moon. The shaved front portion of the head was the sun.

As we all know, the magnetism of the Earth runs between the North and South Poles. There is certainly an effect on the workings of the body when it is aligned with this energy. In Chinese medicine, the Du channel, which runs up the back of the spine to the top of the head, is the primary Yang channel in the body. The Du channel regulates the flow of Yang within the body. The Ren channel continues down from the top of the head to beyond the lower *dan tian* and is the main Yin channel. It controls all circulation of Yin, adjusting its dispersal through the system. The 9 Palaces places a heavy emphasis on combining these two channels into one continuous path, circulating in unison with the breath. This is the Microcosmic Orbit. When the flow of Yin and Yang is united within the body, one can begin to achieve a greater harmony with the Yin and Yang of the universe.

Other important Qi paths that will be addressed in the practice of 9 Palaces Qi Gong are not so directly related to Chinese medicine. They are nevertheless very important energy sectors that are well worth being aware of. There are three central columns of energy that run vertically, the main one through the center of the body and the other two on each side. These columns connect with Heavenly energy, extending beyond the parameters of the physical body. In the 9 Palaces, the emphasis is put upon replenishing the central column with solar energy, while in the Yin practice of the Five Centers Facing the Moon, the side columns and the heart are filled with energy from the moon. Finally, there is a field of energy that enfolds the body from head to toe, encircling it like an envelope. Spinning this cocoon with the light of the sun is the deepest purpose of 9 Palaces Solar Qi Gong.

Though we have presented this information in some detail, when practicing, you don't need to think about centers, columns, and paths. In fact, you don't need to think about anything. Just let your body relax and your mind run free. This is the Taoist principle of going with the flow. The form is set up in a way that will naturally lead you to your goal.

THE HEALTHY AND HAPPY PRACTICE

TRADITIONALLY, 9 PALACES Microcosmic Orbit Qi Gong is broken down into nine levels of practice. Though each level relates to the others, it's imprecise to think that one level of 9 Palaces practice is spiritually or esoterically more advanced than another. Rather, each 9 Palaces form engages a different energetic subsystem in the body in an exchange of energy with the sun. The 9 Palaces Qi Gong covered in this book is also known by the Taoist masters as the Healthy and Happy Practice. It is the first of the nine levels of 9 Palaces practice. Building upon the initial awakening and recognition of the sun's power, this level of the 9 Palaces is primarily focused on physical health and well-being. Each movement is designed to bring the practitioner into a powerful state of wellness. Laid out in three sections, the exercises are arranged to follow a specific sequence of stimulating, detoxifying, nourishing, and then finally connecting the body with the Qi of the sun and the universe beyond. This sequence is optimized to thoroughly cleanse the body and prepare it for reintegration into a higher plane of energy. For certain health conditions, or when time constraints make it impossible to practice the entire form, it is possible to break the 9 Palaces down into separate exercises. However, it is advisable to follow the steps of the form from beginning to end, unless otherwise indicated, to achieve the maximum benefit.

The first section of the 9 Palaces is designed to relax the muscles and stimulate the circulation. You work from the head down to the toes, using a combination of self-massage, gentle neck and spine stretches, and balance exercises that are aided with visualization. After completing this part of the form, all the joints will be loosened and the body will feel warm and comfortable. The wonderful thing about the 9 Palaces, and this portion of the form in particular, is that no matter how stiff and out of shape you might feel, there is no way that you can do these exercises incorrectly, if you are careful to follow them step by step and maintain natural breathing throughout.

You don't have to be in good shape already to do any of the exercises. Whatever condition you are in, 9 Palaces Qi Gong builds you up gently but steadily. This is because unlike many other types of exercise, where attention is paid to a range of motion and to working muscles just past capacity in order to strengthen the body, 9 Palaces Qi Gong puts the importance on how well one combines movement with a natural pattern of breathing. These exercises vigorously tone the muscles of the back, legs, and abdomen, while emphasis is placed on increasing the circulation in the hands, feet, ears, and the blood-rich stomach channels. When the blood and Qi flow are stimulated, oxygen can then more easily reach the muscles. This successfully trains the muscles with considerably less effort. Stimulating the meridians and increasing the circulation is the first step in healing the body.

You will be amazed at how quickly you will start to feel loose and flexible. This is one of the first noticeable benefits of practicing the 9 Palaces. Digestion and sleep are improved. Also, the immune system benefits greatly from the increase in blood circulation. Many people find that after a month or two of practice, they always feel toasty warm even when it's cold out. After a few more months of regular practice, they have substantially raised their energy levels, and common colds and gastric problems become a thing of the past.

Another reason why the warm-up exercises of 9 Palaces Qi Gong are so effective is that on a deeper level, they were designed to harmonize the body's natural rhythm with the rotation of the planet and the energy of the Four Directions. The many circular movements and the gentle swaying and rocking motions attune the body's magnetism with the gravitational force of the Earth, which is also round and spinning. This is the beauty of Taoist Qi Gong. By using a deep understanding of what is most natural for the body and the planet, the simplest techniques can be effortlessly employed.

Harmonizing the body with the forces of nature is further emphasized in the second part of the form. Though this process begins in the warm-ups, the second section moves deeper within the microcosm of the body, as well as opening outward into the universe. Now, along with Heaven and Earth, the practitioner uses the energy of the Five Elements to unblock their corresponding organs and senses.

Our senses are the switching point between the outer world and the internal organs. In 9 Palaces Qi Gong, the route between each organ and its related sense is cleared using static standing postures combined with specific visualizations. First, the Qi of each channel is sent out of the body as far as it can go. Then, once it has reached its furthest limit, good Qi from the universe is brought back through the now opened channel, back into the body. Finally, the palms of the hands are placed over each organ to unite them with the healing warmth of the heart. Again, in the Taoist alchemical texts there are many obtuse references to "Harmonizing the Elements," the "Union of Fire and Water," "Refining the Metals," and so on. The practice of 9 Palaces Qi Gong is the true internal alchemy, grounded in the physical body. The Taoists have long recognized that all change, material, emotional, or spiritual, must come from deep within to be completely solid. With the 9 Palaces, you are using the life force to make changes on a cellular level.

There are physical and psychological explanations for this. The postures and visualizations of 9 Palaces Qi Gong are closely synchronized with the meridians as well as the interaction of the Five Elements. Each standing posture unites the Qi with an organ/sense pathway in a very precise way. Science has explored the changes that occur in brain function when the test subject is simply placed in different positions. However, modern research has only just developed the tools to demonstrate effects that have been studied anecdotally for thousands of years by the Taoist scholars. The visualizations accompanying the postures are also designed for a physical effect. As you practice, you will notice that they are guiding your attention to small muscles and ligaments that normally get little use. Visualizing sending the Qi out gently pressurizes these areas, exercising them isometrically. You are massaging yourself internally with Qi, toning and balancing your body from the inside out. When you build muscle by focusing only on the external effort, it's like forging a steel tube. It's hard, but it's hollow on the inside. Exercising the body by combining Qi with isometrics tones from within. Your core will be as solid as your exterior. This results in deep detoxification and, with practice, an acute sharpening of the senses. The effects can sometimes be quite surprising, but there's nothing supernatural about it. The 9 Palaces Qi Gong simply trains your body's own natural abilities to a level of peak performance.

Once you have warmed up thoroughly and opened each meridian to the universe, the form now proceeds to its finale. The third section of the 9 Palaces is the core of the entire practice, the culmination of the ritual. It is the central ceremony of Solar Qi Gong, as recorded in the canon of the Dragon Gate Sect. At this point, you have prepared yourself to make contact with energy of the sun. You proclaim yourself unafraid, pure of heart, and ready to accept its power into your life. Your nine palaces have been completely cleansed and are ready to absorb Solar Qi.

Not only do you communicate and absorb the sun's energy, by practicing the 9 Palaces, you connect with the unbroken lineage of the masters, for your practice and theirs are the same. This is also the time to unite with and absorb teachings from your ancestors, your God, and your inner guides. Heartfelt practice will bring you support and guidance from all these sources.

Physically and spiritually, you are building up the envelope of life force that surrounds your body. The motions imitate the silkworm, again using circular movements to spin a cocoon of energy around you, one silken thread at a time. The power of the sun is taken into the body. You have created a new balance of the Five Elements, a nascent force within you. One day, when it is ready, it will emerge, a rainbow-colored butterfly of the soul.

BEFORE YOU BEGIN

THROUGHOUT THE YEARS, Dr. Wu has fielded many questions about the practice of 9 Palaces Qi Gong. There are certain very basic ones that come up again and again. The answers to questions such as "When's the best time to practice?" are very variable, depending on the person. They are worth going into in some detail, before you begin to practice.

WHERE TO PRACTICE

WHEN PRACTICING THE 9 Palaces indoors, there are certain things that need to be taken into account, in order to absorb the Qi unimpeded. It's very important to practice on a stone or wood floor. Carpet blocks the Qi. In the monastery, the monks would go so far as to never wear socks, to always allow the soles of the feet to connect with the energy of the Earth. Even now, when you practice, it's best to wear shoes that don't have leather soles. If you feel up to it, you can skip the socks as well. Practicing barefoot isn't necessary. Just make sure your shoes are flat and enclose the foot securely. (Clogs and backless sandals are not good.) Also, comfortable clothes that don't restrict the waist are best. Silk has a special ability to concentrate bioelectricity, but any breathable material is fine. If you would like to add a ceremonial aspect to your practice, by all means wear something that puts you in the right mood. A basic Taoist Feng Shui strategy is to wear the color that corresponds to the season of your birth—green for spring, red for summer, yellow or orange for Indian summer, white for fall, and black for winter. This is to enable you to attract Qi that is most similar to your own.

It is important to understand that practicing indoors is a very poor substitute for outdoor practice. The whole point of 9 Palaces Qi Gong is to unite with nature. It's best to practice the 9 Palaces outside, facing the sun, with a tree that you like behind you and other trees farther away in your line of sight. One of the main objectives of this practice is to gather Qi from the environment. Being outside in the open air, around trees and plants, will surround you with fresh, lively Qi that can be used to nourish the body. Unlike other Qi Gong practices, even including some of the other modes of 9 Palaces, the Healthy and Happy Practice sets up a large two-way pipeline between internal energy and external, environmental energy. Having your feet planted on the earth and the blue sky above your head grounds you energetically. Large quantities of Qi will be able to pass through your body without a physical feeling of overload or an emotional feeling of being overwhelmed. Being indoors, even with hardwood or marble floors, still blocks the flow of Qi that is necessary for maximum healing. Besides receiving a weaker flow of Qi, indoor practice is less rooted by the natural forces you are sharing with, and can result in odd occurrences and spooky sensations.

For the most part, unsettling sensations experienced during Qi Gong practice tend to be related to emotional or physiological processing. This is perfectly natural and is in fact a very positive outcome of serious practice. Our unhappy memories and experiences all too often get lodged in our physical structure. Qi Gong helps to clear the decks and let go of the old baggage. In fact, certain sections of the 9 Palaces form are designed to release a lot of stored-up emotions and remembrances. However, practicing the form in its entirety, from beginning to end without interruption, will provide closure. There is a place to release, a place to renew, and a place to store and settle everything that has come before.

Obviously, some people will be more sensitive to this letting go than others. Daily practice will help process everything you are feeling quickly. For those who are undergoing hardships or difficulties and who feel that even their Qi Gong practice is painful, stick with it. Dr. Wu usually encourages students who are experiencing this to practice twice a day instead of once, to all the more quickly push past the blockages. Keeping a journal when you first start your practice is a great idea. After a few months, you'll be certain to have some interesting stories you will be glad you saved a record of. Practicing with friends is wonderful. There's a lot to share. Nevertheless, in the long run, having a peaceful outdoor environment goes furthest to ensure harmonious practice.

Though in most cases unusual phenomena or sensations while practicing can be chalked up to the mind's need to give form to or pass judgment on unconscious emotional factors, there are times when extraordinary and unexplainable encounters may occur. Because practicing Qi Gong opens the lines of communication between you and many other levels of energy, you might find that occasionally you may receive a visit from a teacher or a relative who has passed on. This is nothing to be alarmed about. Because the 9 Palaces is a Yang practice, it creates a field of living energy that will keep spirits (Yin) from getting too close. At times when Dr. Wu has asked his students to accompany him on Feng Shui purification rituals, he asks them to begin the 9 Palaces while he makes his invocations. Surrounded from all sides with Yang Qi, astral entities and shadowy beings from the realms of the dead will be unable to approach. The 9 Palaces Qi Gong aligns the practitioner with the positive Qi of the universe.

In fact, you may wish to invite teachers or relatives to come to you, to ask an important question or pay them a special honor on an important occasion. For this ritual, you must practice 9 Palaces indoors. Light a pair of red candles and three sticks of incense. Because still water is very Yin, lay out three small bowls of clear water around the room. Then practice as you would normally, with a clear mind, not expecting anything in particular to occur. If your question is meant to be answered, it will be in a way you will know to be true. For certain people who feel constantly oppressed by entities closing in on them, Dr. Wu has suggested laying a table for these beings, with food and drink, and then encouraging them to sit down. Since the essence of Taoist belief is open communication with all things, instead of being afraid, ask them what they want and then try to come to some sort of terms with them. Explaining in a matter-of-fact way that they need to go will usually impel them to leave.

Apart from these very specific rituals, the ideal environment for practicing the 9 Palaces is outdoors, facing the sun. If it's overcast or cloudy, or the sun is blocked from view, you can stand in the direction that approximates its position. You can stand in the shade of a tree or awning. Just make sure your face is turned toward the sun. If facing the sun isn't possible, positioning yourself facing south is a good alternative. If not, stand somewhere that makes you feel comfortable.

Practicing in a location that makes your body feel comfortable and lifts your mood is always best. If you feel good in a particular place, it is because you share the same Qi. The same thing goes for the trees and plants around you. If their fragrance is pleasant and they look healthy, by all means practice with them. Just as a tree releases oxygen into the air, practicing Qi Gong releases good Qi. Just as the environment can help your practice, with the 9 Palaces you are giving something back in return.

It's good to stand in a place where a gentle breeze is blowing. The Qi is carried through the atmosphere on the air currents. A soft feeling of circulation in the air will bring you the highest-quality Qi. Practicing where the air is stagnant or foul-smelling is obviously not a good idea. Practicing where it's too windy is also not good. Too much wind will disrupt the Qi, making it a challenge to absorb it into the body. A very strong draft will blow the Qi away before you can get a chance to use it.

Never practice around garbage. If you see flies swarming about, there is something unclean nearby. Also, practicing near still bodies of water that have no current, such as a swimming pool, cistern, or man-made lake, is not advised. On the other hand, standing beside a flowing river, a waterfall, or the ocean is very purifying. Flowing water cleanses and brings good fortune and opportunities to those who are nearby. Though water is Yin, the force of its current is Yang. Nine Palaces Qi Gong stimulates the Yang Qi to arise within the Yin fluids of the body. This is another way of looking at how the 9 Palaces promotes better circulation and increased bioelectric conductivity.

Practice in your backyard or out at a park. If you live in an apartment building, you can practice on your balcony, though it usually is better to have your feet directly on the ground. In rainy weather, you can stand under an awning, in a gazebo, or on the porch. If it's cold out, put on a coat and a hat. Even in the dead of winter, it doesn't take that long to go through the form. You will find that your body gets very warm during practice anyway. Since this warmth is being generated from inside, the outside temperature won't make that much of a difference. The more you focus your attention on your inner warmth, the less you will notice the weather. In fact, this is a very useful training, so don't be deterred from practicing outdoors, no matter where you live.

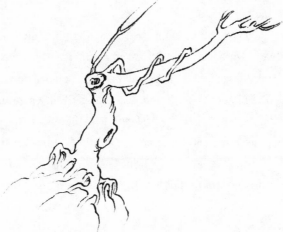

If you have found a location that you like, return there frequently to practice. It's like making yourself a fixture at the local coffee shop. The environment will begin to recognize you and will respond generously with its Qi every time you make an appearance. Coming back frequently will also alert you to any changes that may have taken place. If something feels different and it's not quite as comfortable as it was before, find a new spot. Sometimes the environment has changed, but it is also possible that your own energy has changed. Qi Gong will do that. After a particularly intense practice session, one of Dr. Wu's students wasn't even recognized at first by his own dog. This is nothing to worry about. The 9 Palaces Qi Gong is the most powerful method of refining one's Qi. As you raise yourself to a higher vibrational level, you may have to leave some things behind, but you gain so much more in exchange.

WHEN TO PRACTICE

THERE IS NO set time that is best to practice the 9 Palaces. Depending on what you are trying to accomplish, you must select a time based on a variety of criteria. The single most important rule is that there should be some light available, in order to collect its energy. Of course, sunlight is best. This is not to say that you can never practice 9 Palaces at night. Moonlight is light reflected from the sun. However, daylight is highly preferred. The lunar practice of the 5 Centers Facing Heaven is generally considered the Qi Gong form for nighttime.

Since the 9 Palaces is a Yang form, one of the best general times to practice is between the hours of 11:00 A.M. and 1:00 P.M. These are the peak hours of Yang energy. During these hours, all bodily functions are running smoothly in tempo. The physical abilities, mood, and spirit all operate in unison. The body's energy level is at its highest point in the day. With the sunrise, the strength of the Yang Qi is also steadily rising, until it reaches its peak at noon. Now Yang energy is at its highest level in the external environment. Combining the upward propulsion of the Yang force with the even momentum of the body's workings found now, you can exponentially elevate your energy level with Qi Gong at this time. This is the best time to practice for healing and general well-being.

When Yang peaks, Yin also begins to rise. Sunrise and sunset are very special times, when the levels of Yin and Yang meet in even balance for the day. If you want to harmonize these forces within yourself, practice at daybreak, or when the sun going down paints the sky with beautiful colors. In certain areas, such as Southern California, there are times of year when both the sun and the moon are visible in the sky at the same time. If you ever see this phenomenon, by all means, stop and practice the 9 Palaces.

Early morning also relates to beginnings. If you want to change your fortune or bring new opportunities into your life, get into the habit of going outside to practice when you hear the first calls of the birds. In the Tao, birds are the messengers of Heaven. Big ones, small ones, it doesn't matter. They are all masters of Qi. The ancient Taoist wise men spent much time carefully observing the behaviors of birds. The original divination practices of the *I Ching* were all based on interpreting birds' flight paths. When the birds sing, they are practicing Qi Gong. Practicing along with them can bring you much wisdom and luck. 6:00 A.M. is another special Taoist time for practicing Qi Gong to make changes. In Taoist numerology, the number six represents peace and sacred emptiness. Gentle practicing at six o'clock in the morning will put you in touch with the realization and expression of *wu wei*, this peaceful spiritual void.

Besides these specific times, you can base the best time to practice the 9 Palaces on more personalized factors. One of Wang Xiangzhai's specialties was Hsin I Chuan, a form of martial arts based on the movements of animals. His training style emphasized the Tiger Paw, featuring strength, power, and offensive attack. Therefore, he would practice his standing posture every day from three to five in the morning, known as the Hour of the Tiger. At this time, he could most effectively build up the power and strength of the tiger.

Master Wang confided in the young Dr. Wu the secret to his outstanding string of competition victories. He would always make sure that at least half the matches would be held between 3:00 and 5:00 A.M.—he could then maximize his potential. Besides the fact that his body was acclimatized to that time due to his daily practice, since it was the Hour of the Tiger, he could best utilize the attack force of the Tiger Paw. He would flip his opponents in two seconds and defend his championship title every time.

This story points out the usefulness of personalizing your practice time. The hour of your birth is the best time to combine the Yin and Yang forces within you. This brings out your Original Qi. That is the theory of the Chinese Classics of Internal Medicine. The person you were born into this world as was created by Heaven and Earth. The moment you were born, the best part of you was born—what is most truly You. Your birth time was perfectly timed, generated by that special blend of Yin and Yang that was meant for you alone. Therefore, practicing according to your birth time will provide you with excellent general results. If you were born at 3 A.M. and find it difficult to get up, you can always practice in the equivalent afternoon hour.

No matter what time of day you practice, the most important aspect of 9 Palaces training is that you practice consistently, every single day. You are awakening energies and abilities that normally lie dormant. Just like you have to go to the gym regularly to develop your muscles and keep them in proper tone, daily 9 Palaces Qi Gong is the exercise to stimulate, refine, and enhance your energetic "muscles," each day's practice building on the days before. At least at first, make an effort to practice the entire form daily, preferably at the same time each day. This is the quickest way to make progress in your training. Consistent practice, especially for new students, strengthens and elevates many systems in the body. If you miss a day or two early in your efforts, you will find that your level has dipped back down again and you will have to retread territory you have already covered. It takes time for the body to adjust to the positive changes you are making, before it can stabilize at a higher plateau. Of course, after years of practice, permanent changes in enhanced circulation, hormonal balance, and immune function can be achieved, but even in the short term, significant progress is noticeable. From just seven days of continuous practice, you will gain new ways of seeing and open yourself to fresh opportunities and insights. After forty-nine days, you will reach a further level of capability and self-awareness that will permeate your entire life and the lives of those around you. After a full year of uninterrupted practice, it is said that you will find the true meaning of the

I Ching and understand Heaven. The 9 Palaces is your communication with Heaven, letting its power in. Once you have Heaven's power within you, it becomes your power to influence the world for good and help others. God's truth is everywhere to be found in the universe. This truth is the path to good fortune, no matter your religion or creed. You will find the proof of it within your practice.

MINDSET

TO GAIN MAXIMUM benefit from 9 Palaces Qi Gong, you must enter into your practice with a particular way of thinking and feeling. As it is a practice that takes you deep within yourself, many different emotions, old memories, and body issues might be brought to the surface. This is a natural part of the cleansing process that occurs in serious Qi Gong study. The goal is to reach a new level of energy and self-realization, so along the way, certain things will have to be let go of, whether mentally or physically based. Although it is something to be expected and understood as a natural detoxification, it helps to remember that what needs to be moved on from will pass away in its own time, as a result of your consistent practice. As there is an enormous connection between physical, energetic, and emotional balance, it is good to view your 9 Palaces practice as a path to this harmony, rather than demanding it of yourself before you begin. If you are having a bad day or have a lot of things on your mind, it still is valuable to make the time to practice. You will feel better by the time you are finished. However, it is important to put the stresses and worries of the daily world behind you so that you can practice with undivided concentration.

The ideal mind-set for Qi Gong training can be summed up by the Chinese phrase *Ru Jing, Ru Ding, Ru Wo*. These are three stages of clearing the mind and entering into the perfect receptive state to gain maximum benefit from your practice. *Ru Jing* is the first level. It means letting go of your thoughts, emptying the mind and body of their concerns. You have to empty yourself first, before you can receive something new to replace it with. This is the basic principle of Taoist theory. If you are having trouble putting aside your problems, stop for a moment before you begin your practice. Analyze the issues that are plaguing your mind and find a quick answer for confronting each one. They may be only the most temporary solutions, but understand that they will serve well enough for the time it will take you to do your practice. Finding quick answers like this is a good training for decision making in everyday life. On a deeper level, knowing how to give answers to questions and doubts is a meaningful way of caring for your health. Answer questions, fears, worries, and doubts to regulate the body.

After you have put aside all your thoughts, you stand empty and ready to practice. The next stage is *Ru Ding*. This is the point where you have calmed the spirit and forgotten about the self. Nothing can reach in to bother or affect you. After a certain amount of serious practice, many people are surprised to reach this point in their daily life. They become less emotionally attached to the events occurring around them. This state of mind is referred to as *se kong*, *se* being emotional colors, "the colorful world," and *kong* meaning empty. Whether you achieve this in day-to-day life or just while caught up in the middle of the 9 Palaces, your mind, body, and spirit will benefit from the rest this emptiness brings. After *ru ding* comes *ru wa*. The body regulates with the universe. You forget yourself completely. This is the ultimate experience of harmony and balance. Be aware that there is no need to force oneself intellectually to affect this state of consciousness. It will come naturally as you advance in your training. Practice well, and your efforts will reward you.

Ru Jing, Ru Ding, and *Ru Wa* are natural states that are reached through 9 Palaces practice. They are the result of the integration of the energies and forces of the body. There's no getting around the fact that 9 Palaces Qi Gong requires a certain effort and time commitment to gain results such as these. If after a certain amount of regular practice you find that you still cannot relax, the problem is that you are too involved in relationships. Sex is our nature. Taoism recognizes its inherent power. The Taoist study of sex was absolutely closed off to the public. Among the many schools of Taoism represented at the White Cloud Monastery, a school of sex practice existed into the earlier half of the twentieth century. However, it was highly restricted. Dr. Wu has a funny story of being sent by Master Du with a delivery for the master of the sexual sect. He remembers coming back excited and telling his teacher, "That place was great! They had so many toys there." Master Du scolded the boy, telling him, "I sent you there to deliver a package, not look around."

Taoist sex is very different from what you might think. The Summer Palace, outside Beijing, has a famous mural of sex gods and goddesses. They intertwine in many postures not simply for pleasure, but for cultivation. As a Qi Gong practitioner, see through sex to reach emptiness. Some people can't. They become stuck. There's an old Chinese folk saying: "Women want to be the last one for a man, men want to be the first for a woman." Taoist sex is empty. You cannot get rid of sexual feelings, but you can experience them to reach freedom, instead of being bound by them.

To achieve calmness and clarity of mind and body with Qi Gong takes time and effort. However, there is a simple sitting posture you can try for just five or ten minutes a day that will balance the most important energies, nourish them, and keep them protected from the vagaries of life. Although this meditation is separate from 9 Palaces Qi Gong, we've included it here as something every reader can try, even if there's no time for the more lengthy 9 Palaces form. We encourage every reader to try it for a few days while you read this book. A week's worth of practice will help you to understand the true potential of Qi Gong. Sit upright in a chair, at the edge of the seat so that your back is upright. First put your hands palm up on top of your knees and press the soles of your feet together. Sit in this posture for just a moment to collect your Qi and create a space to practice inside. Then put your feet back on the floor, legs together. Your body should form three exact right angles; feet to knees, knees to hips, and hips to shoulders. These three angles must be formed to practice this exercise correctly. Your legs should be slightly apart and yet kept at the proper angle.

Rest the back of the right hand on the palm of the left hand. With the thumb and first finger of the left hand, encircle the right palm, pressing into the *lao gong* point in the center of the palm with the thumb and its opposite point on the back of the hand with the forefinger. You can find these points by feeling around a bit. The place that is sore or sensitive is the right spot. Hold your hands clasped in this position at the level of the genitals, keeping the arms relaxed and the elbows bent. Touch the tip of the tongue to the roof of the mouth, behind the front teeth. Close your eyes. Shut your eyes off from the outside world. What does that mean? We are always looking out at things. This expends a lot of our own internal energy in the process. Close your eyes and hold in the energy behind them. Feel how the eyeballs naturally want to relax with a sensation of diffusion. Do not let this happen. Hold the sensation of "looking" inward within your eyes, keeping it from dissipating out toward your eyelids. Close off your ears from the outside in this same way. While sitting, hands clasped and contacting the proper points, tongue in place, eyes and ears sealed off, inhale thinly and gently through the nose and exhale through the pores of the skin. If the exhalation is difficult, you can exhale through the nose and the pores together. Feel as if you are sitting at the center of the Immortal Peach, or, in other terms, back inside your mother's womb as you continue to breathe, sealed away in a state of safety and rest. Sit like this for five to ten minutes.

This exercise nourishes the Three Treasures, *Jing*, Qi, and *Shen*. Closing the eyes nourishes *Jing*, which is our essence. The spark you see when you look into a person's eye is the *Jing*. Closing the ears nourishes *Shen*, or spirit. Righteous acts and steady Qi Gong practice can bring out a radiant light surrounding the practitioner. This is *Shen*. Breathing through the skin nourishes Qi, which is the life force within everything. The inner *lao gong* point in the center of the palm is part of the Heart channel. Its opposite point on the back of the hand, the outer *lao gong*, is connected to the Triple Burner channel. The heart point will help regulate the blood flow and circulation. The Triple Burner point regulates the balance and flow of Qi inside the body. When connected together, as in this meditation, a circuit is opened that will regulate the emotions and keep a person steady and balanced. This practice helps prevent heart attacks and blood pressure problems, enhances the immune system and keeps negative Qi from invading the body. To paraphrase the Yellow Emperor's Classic of Medicine: "With positive Qi stored inside, evil cannot interfere. When evil orchestrates its forces, one's Qi must be weak." This simple practice takes only a few minutes and has a wealth of positive results. If you try only one exercise in this book, this is the one to use. It will open your eyes to the meaning of Qi Gong.

Just as a blade of grass will bend in the wind while the mighty tree breaks, this is the ideal achievement in human behavior. Iron and steel can be broken, but water cannot, as much as one tries. We must flow like water, recognizing that this is not weakness. There is enough force within a flood to destroy everything in its path. Even a drop of water can bore a hole in a stone if it drips steadily over the years. This is the 9 Palaces. We are looking for movement within stillness, for the force that surrounds a pristine point of silence. You are sitting or standing perfectly still, but you are exercising, communicating, reaching out nonetheless. The rotors on an airplane spin so fast, they can't be seen. It's as if they weren't moving at all. A submarine deep underwater moves smoothly along, even though the waves are stormy on the surface of the ocean. When you practice Qi Gong, you have to have the same feeling. This is the state the 9 Palaces helps you to reach. The eye of the tornado is perfectly calm, but mighty forces swirl up from its center. In this way, we generate new energy and nourish what lies deep within, in a state of perfect balance.

THREE

Opening the Gates

A FAMOUS TAOIST image portrays the human body in the form of a

landscape, filled with mythical beings, workers, and animals amidst flowing

rivers, jagged mountains, and grassy plains. Meditating on the underlying

meaning of this image raises a profound insight into the search for the self.

Traditionally attributed to Sun Tzu, it was said to have been created by him

in the last years of his life as an atonement for the destruction caused by his monumental *Art of War*. Etched into stone, rubbings and reproductions of it have been made ever since, making it one of the most famous of all Taoist alchemical illustrations. This natural scene peopled with farmers, a spinning woman, a little monkey-boy holding the Great Dipper, and Lao Tze meditating beneath mountain peaks also depicts the physical and esoteric structure of the human body. Perhaps its wisdom lies less in its careful depiction of the body's energy pathways than in its beautiful and peaceful design. To access the soul, one must journey through the inner landscape of the physical body. However, we are assured that this exploration is a wonderful voyage of self-discovery, not a dangerous expedition into the wilds of the unknown. One sees a pastoral scene before the eye, inviting the traveler to wander through its tree-lined groves and ride its clear waters. Having reached the summit, the wise man rests in contemplation. Its great truth lies in illustrating the natural simplicity of the universe that lies within the body.

Exploring the energetic landscape of one's body is one of the true goals of Taoist internal cultivation. The practice of 9 Palaces Qi Gong has been carefully preserved over the generations to help take the first steps down the road on this journey.

9 PALACES QI GONG—SECTION ONE

THE EARS

THE 9 PALACES Qi Gong begins by awakening the body to the flow of Qi. start by standing, feet shoulder-width apart, toes pointed inward to slightly open the pelvis. Make sure your shoulders and arms are relaxed and your chin is gently held in toward the neck. Take your pulse by feeling with four fingers at the wrist or behind the ear. Regulate your breathing to match the pace of your pulse; four beats equal one inhale and the next four equal one exhale. There is no need to slow the heart rate. Whether your pulse is faster or slower, breathe to match its tempo. In this way, your breathing pattern and heart rate will harmonize based on your daily needs. Maintain this breathing pattern throughout the 9 Palaces form for maximum benefit. After you feel comfort-

able, clear your mind by assessing and then letting go of your
cares, reaching *Ru Jing.*

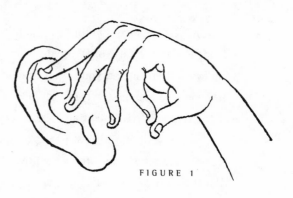

FIGURE 1

The Taoists believe that
when a child is born, the spirit
enters the body with its first
breath. A slap on the bottom
isn't necessary. Just by flicking
the soles of the newborn's feet,
the *hun, shen,* and *po,* or spiritual, human, and animal souls, can arrive.
Arousing the many acupuncture points concentrated on the bottom of the
feet is enough for the different parts of the soul to marry with the physical
body.

For this same reason, 9 Palaces Qi Gong begins with flicking the ears.
After you have regulated your breathing and calmed the mind, the hands
form loose fists with the thumb on top of the rest of the fingers. Running the
thumb over them one by one, starting with the pinkies first, flick your fingers outward in a burst, striking the fronts of the ears. If you flick the fingers
in this way, the fingertips should contact most of the surface of the front of
the ear. (Figure 1.)

The ear is shaped like a fetus. It is a miniature representation of the body,
including all the acupuncture points, meridians, and organs. As a microcosm
of the body, flicking the ears vigorously activates your entire physical structure. This exercise is traditionally considered the first of Lao Tze's original
thirteen Qi Gong exercises. The idea is to flick them with enough force to
make them red, hot, and slightly painful. Don't worry about hurting your
ears. This forceful flicking not only strengthens the cartilage and increases
the circulation, but the sensation of pain will stimulate a surge of endorphins
to the area, allowing the Qi to rush in. By flicking the ears, you are activat-
ing all the points in your body, warming and massaging your organs with Qi.

The pressure points in the ears regulate the Qi and the major bodily
functions. By flicking your ears, you can quickly cure yourself of many types
of illness. In Chinese and Taoist medicine, the ears are related to the kidneys.
If you look at your ears, you will see that they even look like two kidneys. The

kidneys' performance is in turn related to the hormonal balance of the brain. By increasing the flow of Qi in your ears, you are bringing more Qi to your kidneys and enhancing your brain function. Having a direct connection to the endocrine system, strong, healthy kidneys can preserve the youthful balance of the reproductive system and the metabolism, greatly adding to fertility and longevity. Dr. Wu's Taoist uncles back in China have always emphasized their ear practices. They are all well over one hundred years old and are as vital and alert as men half their age.

Besides balancing the hormones, flicking the ears also regulates the brain by increasing the blood circulation. More blood flow to the brain means better memory retention and more capacity for efficient thinking and reasoning. More than any other type of exercise, ear training can prevent the forgetfulness and dementia that often occur in old age. In the short term, improving the circulation in your ears can prevent a variety of colds, flu, and muscle and joint pains. In the Chinese system, catching a cold is not blamed on germs and viruses. It is considered a result of being unable to adapt quickly enough to environmental conditions. Abrupt shifts in the weather can stress the body as it tries to keep up with them. When your ears are warm and there is plenty of fresh blood flowing through their tiny capillaries, your body temperature will be able to remain stable in relation to the temperature outside. You will find that you will be less susceptible to chills and colds. The same thing holds true for muscle stiffness and joint pain when the weather turns cold or rainy. If the warmth of your body is constant, changes in the weather will have less of an effect.

Flick your ears until they are painful and hot. This should take at least fifteen flicks. Remember to flick with the hand cupped in a loose fist, one finger at a time in quick succession. Loose, "hollow" fists allow more Qi to come to the hands. This is the Taoist concept of Emptiness in action. If your fists were clenched shut, how would you be able to get anything into or out of them?

Flicking each finger separately takes a little coordination at first, but it is an excellent way to increase the strength and force of the fingers. As we will see later in this chapter, hand and finger exercises are another very important part of Taoist physical training. Improving the circulation in the ears, hands, and feet fortifies the immune system by holding warmth inside

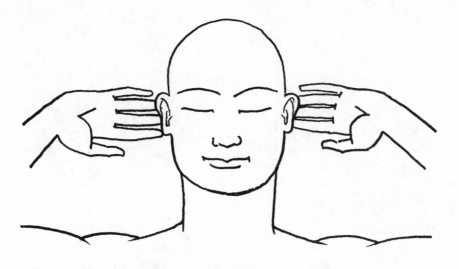

FIGURE 2

the body. Strengthening the fingers has an additional importance due to the major meridians that begin in each of them. By flicking the ears while isolating each finger, you are combining the meridians with all the points in the ear. Simply pull the thumb slowly across each finger. Take your time and go gently. You don't have to use a lot of effort. Remembering to keep your breathing aligned with your pulse will also make this exercise easier and less painful. If it's too difficult to flick the ears in this manner, you can put all your fingers together in a loose cup shape and rub the front of your ears with your fingertips instead. Just remember to only rub in one direction, from the inside of the ears outward. If you don't want to feel the pain, you can flick or rub your ears nine times, but the truth is, this is one of those "more pain, more gain" exercises. Try it and see.

After you flick the ears from the front, with the tips of the fingers cupped together, flick the backs of the ears, rubbing from back to front (Figure 2). Again, don't be afraid to do this vigorously. Flicking the ears from the front and the back together can help to cure many common illnesses caused not only by shifts in the weather but also by infection and weakness of the lungs. As the two main Yin organ networks, the kidney/ear and the lung/nose channels are closely related. For asthma, respiratory infections, and helping to quit smoking, flicking the ears from the front then the back is very

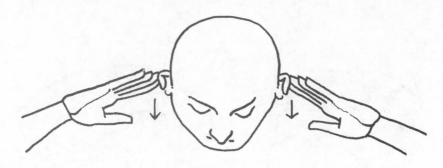

FIGURE 3

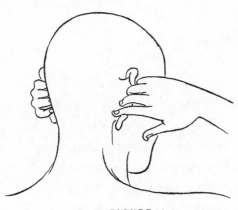

FIGURE 4

effective. If you feel you might be coming down with a cold, try flicking your ears throughout the day, keeping their heat level constant. You will find that more often than not, the cold won't even set in, or if it does, its symptoms will be greatly reduced. This also works very well for ear infections and damage to the eardrums.

As in the front, flick or rub every part of the ear, top, middle, bottom, and inner and outer edge. Bend the ears over to the front as you rub or flick. (Figure 3.) There are special points on the back of the ear that regulate blood pressure (Figure 4). Whether your blood pressure is too high or too low, exercising this part of the ear will help bring it back to a normal level. There are also deeper meanings behind this practice. Flicking the backs of the ears can increase opportunities in your life, because as the Taoists say, behind every event, prospects and opportunities can be found. Sensitizing the ears can help you tune into many possibilities for yourself that you may otherwise have been unaware of (Figure 5).

When Dr. Wu was young, a poor farmer came to the White Cloud Monastery, desperately in need of help. His field had borne a fine harvest, but now he had so much produce that if he couldn't sell it immediately, it would all go bad. He needed to get a certain amount of money for the crop or he and his family would have to choose between going hungry or being turned off their land. Master Du told him to kneel down outside the gates of the monastery and flick his ears until the sun went down and this would bring him the money he needed. Dutifully, he kneeled down

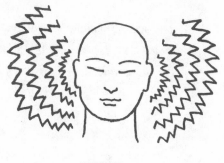

FIGURE 5

and started flicking. He flicked his ears without pause from eight in the morning to six in the evening. By the time Master Du told him to return to his family, his ears were swollen and scraped raw. Two days later, the farmer returned to the monastery bearing an offering of thanks. He had sold his crops at the price he asked for. The Taoists believe that the ears are like twin radar dishes, able to tune in to all the messages of the universe. By honing the body's natural equipment, anyone can lock into this important information.

Your ears are a symbol of yourself. By exercising them, you will be adding many happy years to your life, as well as increasing your opportunities. After

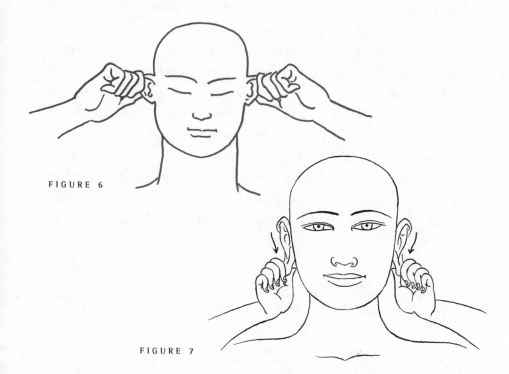

FIGURE 6

FIGURE 7

your ears are thoroughly heated, you can go on to the next exercise. Using your thumb and forefinger, gently squeeze the rims of the ear, pinching them from the top down (Figure 6). When you reach the earlobe, you can finish off with a light pull downward (Figure 7). As you work your way down, gradually go inward, grabbing as much of the flesh of the backs of the ears as you can. This practice is particularly good for regulating blood pressure. Relaxing the body with this exercise can result in a drop in blood pressure of up to ten points. You can test this by testing your pressure, massaging the ears, and then measuring your pressure again. You will see an immediate improvement. In the long term, this exercise can help permanently lower high blood pressure or prevent its occurrence entirely. Repeat the earlobe massage from top to bottom no less than nine times.

As we will see, most of the warm-up exercises in 9 Palaces Qi Gong are repeated in sets of nine. The number nine has a great deal of significance in Taoist philosophy. Nine is the number of Heaven. It symbolizes the fusion of Yin and Yang. In Chinese, the words for *wine* and the number nine are very similar. Just as fine wine mellows as it ages, the number nine represents continuity and good fortune. In both Chinese and Western numerals, nine is the largest integer, containing all the other numbers. After nine, everything goes back to zero and one. In this sense, nine is the symbol of eternity because with it the cycle is completed, finished by returning to its origin.

For the Taoist, nine also hints at the cosmic connection between the microcosm and macrocosm. Just as the nine openings in the body connect to the inner organs and the world outside, there are nine stars that form the conduit for communication between Heaven and Earth. Human and Heaven are one.

The nine openings of the body connect to the nine major organs: the eyes to the liver, the mouth to the stomach and spleen, the ears to the two kidneys, the nostrils to the two lungs, the urethra to the bladder, and the anus to the intestines. One major goal of 9 Palaces Qi Gong is maintaining the free flow of communication between your senses and your organs. Listening to the signals of your body is the most important thing you can do to maintain good health. Your insides are making major decisions for you all day long. Becoming aware of what they are trying to tell you will help you more consciously recognize the best choices to make for your life. An obvious example is to eat lightly if your stomach feels upset, or to get more rest if you feel run down and tired. There are hundreds of subtle cues that are being beamed throughout your body at all times. They affect your decision-making processes and your ability to act. Keeping your nine palaces clean will open up your ability to live in unison with the internal rhythms of your body.

This same principle is at work when the goal is to live in harmony with the universe. There is a special connection between the patterns of the universe and the wishes and aspirations of humanity. Each influences the other in a steady give-and-take. Just as our deepest subconscious drives can determine the events in our lives, cosmic forces from above filter down to us through the stars. For example, birth is expressed through the energy of the Big Dipper and death through the Little Dipper. Developing the ability to read the signposts that the universe holds up for us can give us many clues for living our lives. Remember that just as keeping our nine organs healthy will help us to function correctly in our lives from the inside out, building the abilities of our nine openings will allow Heavenly Qi to reach us in ways that will be much easier for us to understand.

How do we tap into the energy of the stars? It's something that anyone can do, because a piece of each one of us is a star. There is a star in the sky for every person on Earth. Before we are born, we pass through the realms of existence in the form of cosmic particles known as *ling zi* or *ling*. We circulate freely through the stars until the moment of our birth. As our soul enters the material plane, it splits in half. One half stays with us here in the physical body, while the other half remains in the heavens, continuing to mingle with the cosmic energy, or *ling*, of the rest of creation. A Taoist adage muses whether the first cries of an infant express the excitement of finally being released into the world or the trauma of being separated from its other half.

Our destiny is determined by a combination of prenatal (pre-Heaven) and postnatal (post-Heaven) Qi. Some factors and opportunities we bring into our lives are based on choices we have made or avoided. These cause-and-effect occurrences are usually not hard to analyze and make changes to. Some things are predetermined in Heaven and are less obvious to perceive. These pre-Heaven influences are also much more difficult to change. It's not always easy to determine what influences are at work when new events occur. Often they are a result of a combination of prenatal and postnatal Qi. For example, if you catch a cold, it could be because you stayed too long in a drafty place, or there could be a genetic weakness in your immune system. The 9 Palaces Qi Gong helps you to alter your fate in two ways at once. It works on postnatal influences by stabilizing your Qi, shoring it up against outside environmental factors. More important, the 9 Palaces helps correct difficulties involving pre-Heaven conditions by helping you to align with your other half in the sky.

Students have asked Dr. Wu why the navel isn't included in the nine openings of the body. He points out that your navel is created after you are born. The 9 Palaces works on the parts of you that you came into this world with: your Original Self. As we grow older, the aging process, as well as the poor judgment calls and harm we do to others, brings us further and further out of alignment with our other half. By relaxing the muscles and regulating the flow of energy in the body, 9 Palaces Qi Gong reintegrates us, first with our physical body and then with our *ling,* or cosmic energy. Directly connecting with our other half, we are then able to benefit from the universal knowledge that it has absorbed as it commingles with all the *ling* of all other living things.

Your *ling* connects you with universal information. Aligning with your other half also reunites you with ancestors and relatives who have passed away. All Qi carries with it messages. The *ling zi,* or particles of *ling,* have their own Qi. When your body is firmly linked with your ling qi, a beacon of energy is created on the astral plane that can help their blessings and wisdom to find you. In the Taoist worldview, inner guides and heavenly teachers are all part of the same thing: your own connection to the universe. All the guidance you need is very close at hand. As the Taoist saying goes, "Three feet above your head, a god is watching." By developing your Original Qi, the natural energy of your body, you can understand your destiny and change your fate. The messages of heaven will be yours to read.

This might seem like a very lofty goal, but there are actually many simple exercises that can improve your fortune. As we have said, the ears are a symbol of the self. Careful observation of the shape of the ears can be as revealing as a look into someone's eyes. Your inner personality determines the shape and texture of your ears. Stiff ears indicate an opinionated person, someone who has very definite ideas about the way things should be done and sticks by them firmly. Depending on how stiff the ears are, the person can be firm or downright stubborn. Politicians often have stiff ears. Think of presidential caricatures. How many presidents are portrayed with enormous, rigid ears? Even without a background in Taoist physiognomy, the subconscious mind responds to the important cues of the ears.

You want your ears to be flexible. Rigidity leads to death. Exercising your ears by flicking and pinching them tones and softens the ear cartilage, which in turn makes the ears more sensitive to sound changes and subtle vibrations. Flexible ears will help you adjust to the changes in life. However, ears that are too soft are not good. This person can be weak-willed or incapable of independent thought. To build resilience, train the ears. Getting the circulation going will strengthen the personality as well as the tissue.

The ears are related to the kidneys, which are ruled by the element of water. Water symbolizes money, fortune, and good luck. Working on changing the shape of your ears can stimulate change in your life. Long ears point to longevity and good health. When you pinch your ears, be sure to pull down on the earlobes each time you work your way down. Giving them a good tug will lengthen your ears and extend your life. Heart problems are revealed by wrinkles on the ears. Round ears signify wealth. Thick ears indicate good fortune and many blessings. The Buddha is often portrayed with large ears and thick, pendulous earlobes. This is an invocation of blessings, material comfort, and long life. The inner meaning of this common image is based on the study of the ears.

Don't think these are just old wives' tales. Dr. Wu observes the ears of each of his patients. The bankers, accountants, and businessmen usually have round ears. The older patients' ears are much longer than their younger counterparts'. Dr. Wu has found that these indicators are true nearly 90 percent of the time. Make your own study by observing the ears of your friends and acquaintances.

Women, in particular, can be well interpreted by the condition of their ears. The Dragon Gate Classic texts recommends that women should wear large, dangling earrings to maintain their health. Even Western chiropractors recognize that pulling down on the ears helps to loosen crucial nerve networks that, when cleared, allow toxins to release and impulses to the brain to flow more freely. Remember that there is always a two-way connection between the outer world and the inner realms. Working on your external appearance will reflect your internal health just as surely as healing your insides will change your outer appearance.

The third ear exercise also enhances the ability to hear the messages of heaven. Softly cupping the hands, place the palms over the ears, with the fingers resting on the back of the head and the elbows pointing out (Figure 8). Using a gentle pressure, press the palms over the ears, forming a light seal. Press in slightly and then release the hands quickly a few inches away from the head, popping open the seal (Figure 9). The object here is to create a suction effect over the ears to open and balance the ear canal. This is the same prin-

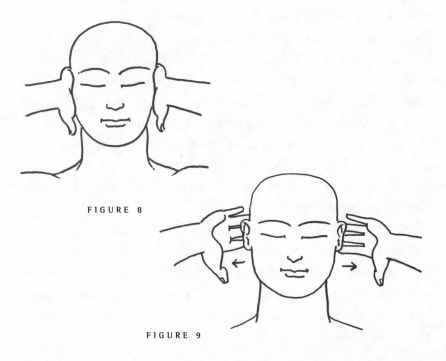

FIGURE 8

FIGURE 9

ciple as using a plunger to unblock a backed-up toilet. Using suction to readjust the difference in pressure around the clog loosens it and allows it to flow through. Don't use a lot of force when you press the ears. Just feel the suction take hold and then pull the hands away smoothly. Repeat nine times.

The ears operate on the same principle as a radar dish. Sound waves are collected in the cupshaped opening of the ear, pass through the coils of the ear canal where they are concentrated, and then strike the eardrum. By resonating off the thin membrane of the eardrum, sound waves are translated into vibrations that stroke the sensitive nerve bundles of the inner ear. After receiving this physical stimulation, the nerve impulses are then sent along to the brain, where they are converted into the experience of sound.

Although humans are superior to animals in many ways, our animal friends have preserved and enhanced abilities that we have let slip. Most animals depend on their sense of hearing to detect danger and hunt for food. Some have adapted in even more unusual ways. The bat uses its highly developed sense of hearing in combination with the call of its voice to "see" the world around it. Its ears are sensitive enough to detect the speed at which the vibration of its high-pitched squeaks bounces back off of objects in the environment. The bat paints a picture of the landscape with sound.

Humans have built machines that imitate this ability. With sonar and ultrasound, we can pilot submarines and look into the body. Nevertheless, we all have the ability, through the practice of Qi Gong, to bring out the full potential of our senses without depending on machines. The greatest reward of 9 Palaces Qi Gong is its ability to bring health while actualizing the amazing capabilities of the body. The single thing that has separated people from their original abilities has been the lack of a system to effectively develop them. With this complete discussion of 9 Palaces Qi Gong, the tools have been revealed at last. They are simple and easy to use. They are here for you to try.

The suction effect of the ear-plunging exercise opens the ear canal, dislodging accumulated debris in the ear ducts as well as in the canal itself. Not only is the eardrum opened; the energy channels that connect the ears to the kidneys are cleared. In the Chinese system, the kidneys are the source of the energy that powers the ability to hear. This is why as people age and their kidney function is depleted, the ability to hear also decreases. By keeping the connection between ear and kidney unblocked and free of residue, the primary cause of age-related hearing loss is kept at bay. Earaches, sinusitis, and tinnitis, or ringing in the ears, can be effectively reduced with this exercise as well. Since every channel is a two-way street, unblocked ears bring larger quantities of Qi into the kidneys from the outside, alleviating any deficiency that might be present without resorting to medicines and herbs.

The inner ear maintains the body's sense of equilibrium. By regulating the pressure levels within the ear, the suction exercise substantially enhances one's balance and center of gravity. This is a great boon for the elderly and anyone in a physical rehabilitation program. Dizziness, nausea, motion sickness, and feelings of shakiness and instability when standing or walking are all vastly improved by repressurizing the inner ear. Regular practice can make permanent changes in the ear's ability to withstand subtle as well as extreme changes of pressure. I can personally attest that the intense discomfort that air travel can cause upon takeoff and landing can be completely eliminated with steady practice of the ear suction exercise. For years after a serious ear infection, any airplane descent, no matter how short, would completely block my ears, causing dizziness, sharp headache, and nausea. None of the tips for popping the ears such as chewing gum or yawning had the slightest effect. I had to count on at least three or four hours of complete incapacitation before the symptoms would clear. After less than three months of plunging my ears, nine repetitions a day, my problem was completely gone, never to return.

This exercise dramatically improves one's sense of hearing by unblocking the ear canal and stimulating the eardrum. The ears become sensitized not only to a wider range of sound, but to a broad spectrum of pure vibration, at times much lower or higher in frequency than audible sound waves. The natural abilities of animals to sense motion through vibration or subtle changes in the weather through minute adjustments in air pressure are our abilities as well. For the Taoists, the ears are also capable of receiving impressions from the universe that are impossible to measure scientifically, but nevertheless have the ability to manifest as sound, vision, feeling, and sensation. The student of Taoist Qi Gong, beginner or advanced, understands that

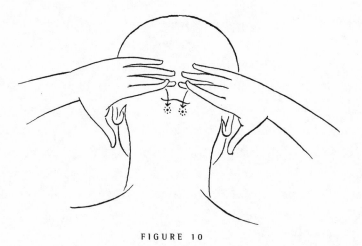

FIGURE 10

achievements that seem impossible or miraculous are simply natural functions of the senses and organs. The beauty of 9 Palaces Qi Gong is that their attainment is so very simple. The only effort required is a commitment to regular practice and a willingness to let go of preconceptions of what we can or can't do. The messages of heaven are there for the listening.

The final ear exercise is known as "Beating the Heavenly Drum." With the hands still pressed firmly over the ears and the fingers resting on the back of the head as in the ear suction exercise, cross the forefingers over the middle fingers and then flick down with them onto the soft spot at the base of the skull (Figure 10). Repeat nine or thirteen times.

The soft tissue at the base of the skull is considered a crucial point that benefits from strengthening, both in Chinese and Western medicine. From a Western perspective, this part of the body needs to be kept relaxed and properly aligned as the first step to proper posture. It is located directly at the juncture of the skull and the first spinal vertebra. Within this bony casing lies the terminal nerve bundle of the spinal cord as it leads into the base of the brain. Any tightness or obstruction here will restrict the blood flow and nerve impulses to and from the brain. Misalignment at the very top vertebra can result in overcompensation in the position of the jaw, the muscles of the face, and along the length of the spine, which leads to poor posture, pain, and fatigue. In time, more serious conditions such as bone spurs, disk problems, and compromised immune function can develop if not addressed.

Remember that a properly aligned spine results in a healthy nervous system, which in turn elevates all other functions of the body.

In Chinese medicine, this point is referred to as the *feng fu* point, or "wind gate." This point is related to the "small brain," a combination of the brain stem and cerebellum. Generally, Qi Gong treatment of this point is more effective than acupuncture. The small brain directs a wide range of basic body functions. The cerebellum controls balance and coordination. Treating the *feng fu* point can resolve balance problems and certain motor skill disorders, such as slurred speech or difficulty standing upright. The medulla oblongata, located within the brain stem, is in charge of cardiovascular function and the ability to awaken from sleep. Insomnia and heart problems of all kinds, including blood pressure irregularities, are all treatable using the *feng fu* point.

The medulla oblongata also regulates breathing. The ancient Chinese believed that the lungs governed exhalation and the kidneys, inhalation. The controlled breathing of Qi Gong automatically strengthens the connection between the lungs, kidneys, and medulla oblongata. By practicing 9 Palaces Qi Gong, one begins to gain mastery over body functions that are normally considered automatic and uncontrollable. Pressing, tapping, and massaging the *feng fu* point all stimulate the dense package of nerves that connect with this primal part of the brain.

The Taoist perspective on flicking the *feng fu* point is as multifaceted as this part of the body itself. There are amazing tales of Dragon Bones, or *she li zi*. These are relics of saints and high practitioners, kept in secrecy for the miraculous spiritual power they possess. In fact, these relics are the bones of these masters of cultivation, which have undergone a physical transformation, their structure altered by years of intense training and ethical behavior. Dr. Wu had the honor of accompanying the vice chairman of the Buddhist Association of China to the Famen Temple near Xian, repository of one of the few relics of Sakyamuni Buddha in mainland China. Though the vice chairman was a government appointee, he had been sent on a religious mission to this famed temple at the behest of his own spiritual master, the Zhen Guo Fashi Da. As part of his serious religious assignment, he was there to worship Sakyamuni's bones. Though some reliquaries are on display to the public, the vault where the Buddha's finger lies in an ivory box is not open to the public. After he performed his veneration before the relic, the vice chairman asked the abbot who was presiding during the ritual if he would open the box. As he had been personally sent by the Zhen Guo Master, the abbot agreed to open it for him and Dr. Wu. As soon as the lid was lifted, the unlit underground crypt was suffused with a silvery glow, like moonlight. Dr. Wu felt suddenly able to see into his body and the bodies of his companions. Every organ was illuminated and perfectly visible. He was further astounded by the fact that the vice chairman had seen the very same thing. It was a spiritual encounter he can never forget as long as he lives.

How can you describe an impossible experience like this? There certainly aren't any scientific means of duplication or testing. The world of Qi Gong is filled with unexplainable events. Afterward, the abbot told them that far from being the first time this had occurred, every time they had uncovered the relic the same magical light came pouring out. Because Sakyamuni's cultivation was so deep and his belief so great, he had absorbed everything there was into his body. Even after death, his remains were able to reflect back some of this power. Practice Qi Gong with a spirit of complete openness, complete willingness to absorb all the universe has to give. Take it in with all your heart. You will transform yourself in ways you never have dreamed.

The development of *she li zi* is attributed to this practice of flicking the *feng fu* point, which is also known as *She Li Gong*. The Taoist name for the base of the brain is the "ghost gate." This point is considered very vulnerable; sickness, evil, and ghosts all enter the body through here. Have you ever noticed how easy it is to get sick or feel "out of it" after a car accident? Usually, feeling back to normal comes quite a while after the pain has subsided. There is definitely some truth to that sensation of "cold chills on the back of the neck." The body instinctively perceives danger through this spot. By doing this exercise, the practitioner seals the ghost gate. Flicking exactly nine or thirteen times is a warning signal, preventing negative energies from coming near. Strengthening the ghost gate transforms it into the "jade pillow," a primary opening into the body for Heavenly Qi.

By stimulating the nerves at the point where they attach to the brain, the nervous system is sensitized at its root. This increased sensitivity allows the body to operate smoothly as one totally integrated unit. Once reconnected to itself, the body can then connect with the universe in a new way. This is the principle of "as small as no inside, as big as infinity" put into action in the most fundamental way. Qi Gong reorganizes brain chemistry and neural function. There is no question that this produces a shift in perception. Practicing Qi Gong, you begin to see the world in a different light. Though the experience of this change is as individual as the practitioner, a higher level of health will always result in a revitalized awareness of life. Your ears are key jumping-off points for entry into this new world of consciousness and longevity. Even if you practice 9 Palaces strictly for health, without an esoteric or spiritual goal, be prepared for a new level of peace and harmony. It's coming from inside your self.

THE NECK

"Banging the Heavenly Drum" is a double exercise, working on the ears and the neck at once. In their quest for longevity, the ancient Taoists recognized the joint role of the ears and neck in unleashing the power of the brain. Taking their cues from nature, they carefully observed the long-lived animals of land and air, emulating the wisdom of their behavior. In the sky, the eagle is renowned for its acute hearing, eyesight, and intelligence, in addition to its life span, which often stretches well over one hundred years. On land, the tortoise lives to a greatly advanced age and is the ultimate Taoist symbol of longevity.

The Taoists accurately assessed that the common trait shared by the tortoise and the eagle is the strength and flexibility of their necks. The eagle uses its powerful neck muscles to maneuver while diving at great speed for its prey. The turtle's neck thrusts out and retracts into its shell with slow, sturdy ease. The ancients made the connection that a strong, flexible neck would bring them the abilities and long life of these noble creatures. The Taoist principle of learning from the small, recognizing the value of small things, reaps many rich rewards.

Of course, today, both Western and Eastern medicine recognize the importance of a healthy neck for total well-being. As mentioned before, all the nerves tightly bundle into the base of the brain, emerging from the top of the spine. This area needs to be kept open and aligned in order for the nerve impulses to properly flow to and from the brain. Very basic bodily functions, such as breathing and blood pressure, are controlled from the brain stem. Any degeneration here will negatively affect the body over time. A stiff neck will lead to all sorts of pain in the body and head. However, a loose, flexible neck will not only improve your health, but in the Taoist perspective will greatly contribute to your good fortune as well.

Dr. Wu closely observes the posture and carriage of each of his patients. In another example of Taoist physiognomy, the position and bearing of the head on the neck indicates the potential for success. A man who walks with his neck erect and chin and eyes lowered is destined for achievement. Accomplished women, on the other hand, keep their chins held high and their eyes looking straight ahead, neither lowering nor shifting them to the left or right. A person, male or female, who walks hunched over, with the neck contorted and compressed, is heading for difficulty in his or her career. This might seem pretty obvious, but there are actually many deep levels of meaning attached to this basic truth.

There have been times when patients approach Dr. Wu to have their fortunes read. Usually Dr. Wu tells them, "Instead of a reading, how about coming in for a few neck treatments?" Working on their necks, returning them to alignment and proper Qi flow, gives his patients much more in terms of health, increased energy, and positive outlook than any fortunetelling ever could. In his studies, Dr. Wu has found that there is a direct relationship between neck problems and outside difficulties in life approximately 87 percent of the time. If you want to change your fate or your career or accomplish something special, start by exercising your neck. There is great wisdom in changing your appearance to change your life, if the change starts from within.

The first neck exercise is basically a neck self-massage. Starting at the base of the skull, squeeze as much of the width of the back of the neck as you can between the heel of the palm and the fingers of the right hand. Squeeze the flesh of the neck in the hand, working your way down to slightly below the juncture of the shoulders and neck (Figure 11). For a deeper mas-

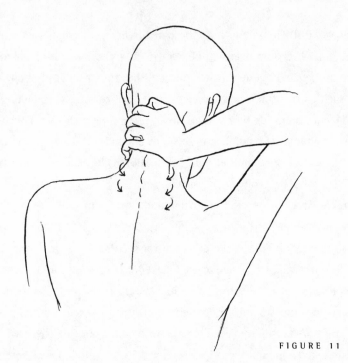

FIGURE 11

sage, tilt your head slightly to the right as you squeeze your way down, pressing into the side of the spine with the tips of the fingers. Repeat nine times, then switch hands and repeat nine times more, using the left hand on the other side of the neck. Again, for a deeper massage, tilt the head slightly to the left and dig into the right side of the spine with the fingertips of the left hand.

Don't forget to keep the breathing even with the pulse. Important acupuncture points are located on either side of the spine. Also, down the length of the spine, the nerves that govern every part of the body extend out from the spinal cord, protected in the center of the vertebrae. However, the point of this neck massage is not so much to break down muscle tension by kneading out knots and tissue accumulation, as is common in Western styles of massage. The main object of this Taoist massage is to warm the neck and increase blood circulation in the area. Once the circulation has been improved, the muscles relax on their own. With further practice, the body can stabilize itself against external pathogens and weather fluctuations. An illness accompanied with a stiff neck is much more difficult to treat than when the neck is soft and warm. With a supple neck, you will find it much easier to stay healthy and keep sickness out.

After entering the body, Qi accumulates in the joints, and especially along the sides of the spine, where there are also many acupuncture points and nerve centers. When practicing Qi Gong or martial arts, the rotation of the joints routes the Qi through the body. In the White Cloud Monastery, the test of a martial artist was based not on quickness, agility, or strength when performing a set or form, but on how effectively each joint was used to direct the Qi. When practicing Taoist neck exercises, do not strain past what is comfortable for you. There is no need to press or squeeze the neck until it hurts. Just lightly grasp the neck in the hand and give it a gentle press. Holding your concentration primarily on the breathing pattern (four beats = one inhale, four beats = one exhale) will allow more Qi to flow into your spine. Let your breath and the Qi do the work, not the muscles in your hands. This way, you will finish your massage with nice, warm, loose muscles, not cramped hands and a sore neck.

Again, this ties in with the concept of *kong*, or emptiness. The idea of creating receptivity and awakening change by emptying out first is a fundamental principle of Taoist thought. The Taoists think of the body as a teapot, with the head as the lid. You have to be able to lift up the lid in order to pour the water in. Opening up the body to allow universal Qi to flow in is the primary goal of 9 Palaces Qi Gong. The 9 Palaces ear and neck exercises clear debris and blockages in the head and spine, allowing the brain to function more efficiently. Increased blood and Qi supply keeps the muscles relaxed, preventing excessive wear on the vertebrae. In this way, massaging the neck, in particular, can help check the buildup of bone spurs and disk erosion. Keeping your neck supple and warm is the Taoist route to longevity.

Transforming your body into an empty vessel is a very deep practice, simply done. Opening yourself up permits you to be filled with the Qi of Heaven and Earth. The first step on the road to complete communication with the universe is to allow the microcosm of the body and the macrocosm of everything outside it to merge. The *I Ching* assigns the three solid bars of the Qian, or Heaven, trigram to the head because the head is considered related to Heaven. In fact, the head itself is a map of the Earth, broken down into three

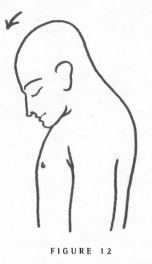

FIGURE 12

regions: above the eyebrows is Heaven, from the eyebrows to the indentation above the lip is Human, and from the lip indentation to the chin is the Ocean. The movement of the neck and head is therefore seen as the movement of Qian and Kun, or Heaven and Earth. The next two neck exercises are very basic, but from a Taoist point of view, they do more than merely stretch the neck. They align the entire body with the Four Directions and the magnetism and motion of the planet.

Remembering to breathe in sync with the heartbeat, stretch the neck out and down as far as it can go, pressing the chin into the chest. Use a little strength here. You want to really feel the chin flattening into the chest (Figure 12). This stretch opens the muscles all the way from the back of the neck to the top of the head and back to the chest. Squeezing firmly into the chest with the chin keeps the spine and back muscles evenly aligned and shoots an extra burst of energy to the brain. With practice, you will feel the muscles of the entire back opening up at this point, sometimes even all the way down the back of the legs to the heels.

In the Chinese system, the heart is considered the true mind. The brain acts as a tool of the heart, carrying out its wishes. Your neck must be kept clear to maintain communication between the heart and the brain. If you have a lot of stiffness or can't bend your neck easily, you may be cutting off the blood circulation to the brain. This exercise is wonderful for brain maintenance. It can help preserve the memory function well into old age. With regular practice, an older person can stay as sharp as someone thirty years younger. A common result of practicing the 9 Palaces is a feeling of energy and alertness. Most of Dr. Wu's students notice a definite increase in their ability to learn and retain new information. All this relates to improved blood circulation in the brain. Conversely, if a patient has symptoms of memory loss, fatigue, dizziness, and high blood pressure, this neck exercise should immediately be added to his or her health care regimen.

People who sit all day at a computer should practice this stretch

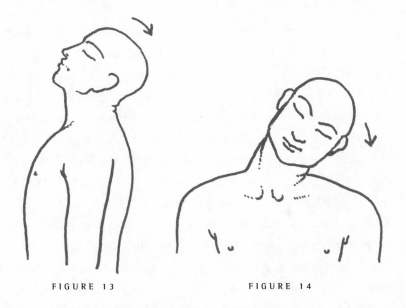

FIGURE 13   FIGURE 14

throughout the day to reduce the fatigue of staring at a screen for long periods. Also, women who love to wear high heels should do this exercise every day. Wearing high heels on a regular basis is a surefire way to throw the back out of alignment. Counteract their effect by bending your head down to your chin. The Taoists don't believe that keeping your chin held high should necessarily be a part of daily behavior. Bowing the head can be more effective. Just like a blade of grass can withstand a strong wind, maintaining a flexible neck can help overcome the storms of life. As the Tao Te Ching points out, the only thing that cannot be bent or broken is water.

After stretching the neck down, stretch the neck up, tilting the head slightly back as you stretch upward (Figure 13). Try to lift up the entire neck, not just the chin. Feel the connection between the muscles of the upper chest and the neck as you lift. Do not hold the breath. Stretch only as far as your breath will allow you, feeling the throat curve forward. The object is not how deeply but how gently you can stretch, letting the breathing and the Qi relax the muscles. Hold only as long as it takes for the tension to release, about a second. Holding for any longer will actually just retighten the neck. Next, tilt the head from the neck over to the left shoulder, then to the right (Figure 14). Make sure to keep the shoulders down. This stretch must be done fluidly, following the rhythm of the breath.

These four stretches, one down, one up, one left and one right, equal one set. From a Taoist point of view, you are bowing to Heaven and Earth. Repeat for nine sets of four. Practiced in this particular order, you are connecting the magnetism in your body to the gravitational pull of the Earth. If a patient complains of insomnia, the first thing Dr. Wu will ask about is the position of his or her bed. He recommends repositioning the bed so that the head lies to the north and the feet point south. With this placement, the body is aligned with the north-to-south magnetism of the polar axis. This usually works for most people. If not, the bed can be placed based on the direction correspon-ding to the season of one's birth. For example, if you were born in the spring, have your bed running east/west with your head to the east. East is the direc-tion related to spring. If you were born in the summer, have your head to the south. Fall is west, and winter is north.

Harmonizing with the currents of energy that transverse the planet is a very basic way to reduce stress on the body. Your body's own currents can flow with greater ease when they flow in the same direction as the energy that sur-rounds them. Four-legged animals often sense impending earthquakes and storms. This is due to the lack of pressure on their spines, which they carry par-allel to the ground. If you have back pain or have experienced a trauma to the internal organs, Dr. Wu suggests crawling on all fours for ten minutes every morning, to ease the viscera and take the weight off the spine. You might feel silly doing this, but it's actually very relaxing. With a comfortable, properly balanced spine, humans can recover the sensitivity to impending weather conditions that the animals never lost. It's one of the many natural abilities 9 Palaces Qi Gong can help you to regain. Don't force it. Try to keep your shoul-ders down and your arms hanging lightly at your sides. Let the Qi do the work. Paradoxically, the less effort you push your muscles to expend, the sooner you will see noticeable improvement in flexibility.

After nine sets of stretching to the Four Directions, move on to the next exercise. Roll the head to the left, chin turned toward the shoulder. Continue rolling down over the chest, to the right chin pointing right, then loosely to the back (Figure 15). Roll the head in this clockwise direction nine times, then reverse and do nine rolls counterclockwise. The key point is to turn the chin to the shoulders as they pass them. Maintain the proper breathing rhythm.

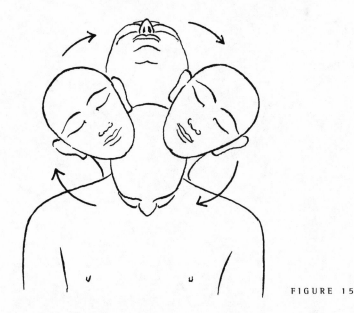

FIGURE 15

As in the rest of the neck exercises, gently controlled breathing is more important than how far you can stretch.

Just as the previous exercise connects the body to the magnetic patterns of the Earth, these neck rolls coordinate you with the Earth's rotation. For a Taoist, in some senses the Four Directions have little importance. Since the planet is constantly rotating under our feet, we never really are standing in the same spot from moment to moment. We might think we are facing south, but in reality, we are spinning at great speed, right along with the Earth beneath our feet. Only because the Earth is so large and we are so small, we don't notice we are moving. The 9 Palaces Qi Gong equalizes our bodies with the centrifugal force that keeps us pinned to the ground. Contacting this envelope of circular energy is the first step toward taking control of its potential power. We will discuss this concept in greater depth throughout this book. For now, reflect on the image of a mighty tornado. The force of its funnel can lift a building off its foundations. Meanwhile, at the center of its power, all is perfectly still—the eye of the storm. The practice of 9 Palaces Qi Gong takes this concept far past an abstract philosophical ideal. With it, you make this transformation a reality within your body.

The next neck exercise should be done carefully. Here, especially, it's

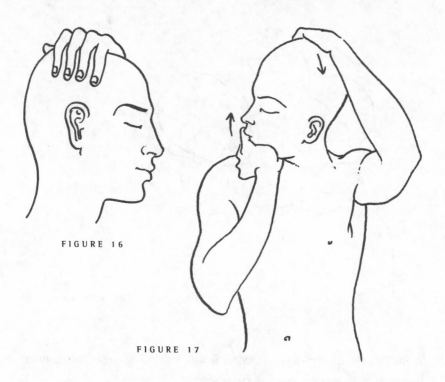

FIGURE 16

FIGURE 17

important to proceed gently, without forcing the muscles. Reach your left hand up and place it on the head. Rather than centering your palm at the very top of the skull, position it over to the right side, the tips of the fingers just over the top of the ear and the side of the hand near the hairline (Figure 16). Hold on to your head with this hand, feeling energy radiating from the center of the palm into the brain. While your left hand is protecting your brain, the right hand comes up under the chin, cupping it with the soft mound at the base of the thumb. Keeping the jaw relaxed, with the mouth slightly open, tug the head down three times very lightly to the right, while pushing up ever so slightly with the hand at the chin. Still supporting the head, straighten the neck and switch hands slowly, bringing the right hand to the left side of the head and the left hand under the right side of the chin. As the hands move into position, at the point where they are parallel with each other at the sides of the head, softly close and then release them, flicking all the toxins and built-up tensions off of the fingers. Alternate from side to side for nine sets (Figure 17).

Key points to be aware of with this stretch include, in order of importance: keeping the upper hand to the side of the skull, cradling it securely while sending energy into the brain; never trying to tug the head farther than it can easily go; keeping the jaw and lips relaxed; and remembering to flick the hands as they circle around to the other side of the head. Though this exercise might seem like a neck stretch, stretching the neck is its least important feature. By keeping the mouth slack while maintaining a firm grip on the widest area of the head, your three soft tugs will stretch all the muscles of the scalp. It isolates and elongates the area between the temples and the top of the jaw. This releases pressure all around the face, eyes and jawline. Tension and poor posture easily distort the point where the jawbone connects with the skull. This can result in pressure headaches, teeth grinding, and decreased sensory capacity in the ears, eyes, and nose. This stretch, done carefully, with attention paid to its subtle details, can relax this area rapidly, preventing chronic conditions such as TMJ (Temporo-Mandibular Joint) dysfunction from setting in.

While loosening key muscles and joints, this stretch also disperses unwanted energy and nourishes the brain. Remember that the centers of the palms are two of the five heart centers in the body (the others being the centers of the soles of the feet and the heart itself, whose energy radiates from a point corresponding with the middle *dan*). Throughout the 9 Palaces, we use the energy of the heart centers to warm and replenish the body. Allowing the impulse to originate in the heart, send its healing energy across the chest, through the arms and out of the palms. If you don't feel it at first, rest assured that with practice it will come as easily and quickly as the thought forms in your mind.

The points over the temples are also important valves between energy stored inside the head and Qi from the outside environment. Keeping the temples clear is very relaxing, mentally and physically. By the time the average person reaches forty, bone spurs have appeared in the neck due to gravity, aging, and anything less than perfect posture. This stretch prevents their worsening. With long-term practice, this stretch loosens what the Taoists consider the joints in the skull. Normally these sutures solidify quickly in childhood. By the time we reach adulthood, they have fused completely. As you increase the level of Qi inside of the body, these joints, as well as others

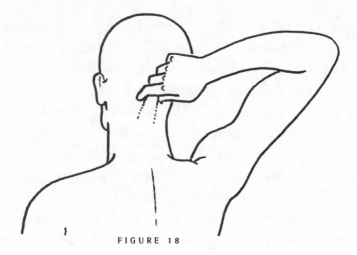

FIGURE 18

in the pelvis and base of the spine, can be pushed back open, creating sensations of lightness and release that can be ecstatically pleasurable. Remember, Qi is stored in the joints, even those we haven't been able to utilize as such since childhood. It just takes practice. Your breath aligned with your heart will bring you all the Qi you will need.

To finish the neck exercises, return to the soft skin at the base of the skull. Grasp the flesh between the thumb and fingers of the left hand (Figure 18). This area can be very tight, but hold on firmly and try to get a good grip. Pinch the skin with the fingers and pull it out, away from the body. Repeat nine times with each hand. This may not be easy. Very often, eye problems such as astigmatism and glaucoma can stiffen this spot. Working on this spot will help maintain healthy eyesight. It lowers eye pressure and can reduce redness and burning. Dark circles under the eyes indicate weakened Qi. Pinching the back of the neck can help you recover quickly. It can also temporarily solve problems with the blood supply to the eyes.

If your neck is particularly tight here, you will be running into difficulties beyond the eyes. As mentioned, this area is the portal of the Ghost Gate. In his years of working in the emergency care clinic in the National Hospital in Beijing, Dr. Wu saw many patients close to death. At times they would get very lively remembering many things that had happened to them, the color returning to their faces as the memories flowed back. However, the backs of their necks would become as hard and unyielding as marble. This was the sign of their imminent death. All life and death can be read in the neck. Nurturing your neck will bring rewards more precious than gold.

THE SHOULDERS

Working our way down the body, the next exercise focuses on the shoulders, back, and spine. Each vertebra houses a series of nerves that connect to the organs and muscles. Many important acupuncture points are ranged on either side of the spine. In this exercise, we are going to twist the spine to open these points, allowing Qi to flow in and energize the entire body system.

Cross the arms and grasp the shoulders firmly, with the fingers holding onto the back (Figure 19). Keep the elbows slightly elevated. The hands and fingers should be placed close to the neck. They need to lie straight back, not angled out to the edges of the shoulder, in order to maintain their best hold and to stabilize the neck. The chin should be kept tucked into the neck at all times, to further stabilize the area. Lean forward at no more than a forty-five-degree angle. This is the beginning posture.

When Dr. Wu teaches his students, he takes them through a progression of stages when introducing certain exercises. This is one of the important reasons to study Qi Gong seriously with an enlightened master. A wise teacher can assess the physical and energetic condition of his students and tailor the training to gently open their bodies to greater and greater levels of Qi. Often, the first stages of a practice can involve more physical exertion in order to unblock and strengthen the channels. In the later stages, when the body is already open, the physical difficulty decreases to focus on gently concentrating the Qi and releasing the mind into the cultivation. To get the most

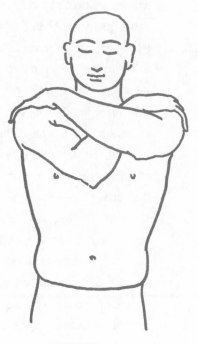

FIGURE 19

out of the 9 Palaces, at times we will break certain exercises down into stages to more fully convey the experience of learning progressively with a teacher. However, if you prefer, it's perfectly acceptable to skip the initial practices and go straight to the final form. One of the most exceptional properties of Taoist Qi Gong is that no matter what physical shape you are in, the exercises are self-regulating. When you practice 9 Palaces, the postures will naturally conform to your ability level, preventing injury and unnecessary strain. This is because the form comes from your own interpretation of it.

Whenever multiple exercises are presented, practice the first level for forty-nine days before moving on to the next level. Forty-nine days, one week short of two cycles of the moon, is a special Taoist initiatory time period. Practice straight through without missing a day, and on the last day you will see that you have gained something very new. What happens is different for every person. Try it and see what you can learn.

The first level of the back exercise puts the emphasis on stretching open the spine and rib cage. While bending at a forty-five-degree angle, twist the torso as far as it can comfortably go to the left (Figure 20). Keep your forward leg slightly bent at the knee to support the body as it turns. Once the torso has turned to its limit, continue twisting the upper torso upward to the left, letting the left elbow lead. Rotate as high as the body's limits will permit. Hold at the top of the stretch for no more than a fraction of a second, then twist the upper torso up in the other direction, letting the right elbow lead. Remember that the body is still turned to the left as this is being done. Finish by twisting the left elbow back up and then straighten the back slightly and twist to the right. Keep twisting to the right, this time allowing the right elbow to lead the torso up (Figure 21). While still facing right, swing down, then up with the left elbow and finish with a final twist led by the right elbow. Turn back to the center, then lift up from the pelvis, stretching the whole torso upward, again leading with the elbows. Keep the chin tucked solidly into the neck to prevent any excess curvature in the spine. Hold for just a moment, then bend down, making sure the chin is still tucked and the back is flat (Figure 22). Do not bend down further than a forty-five-degree angle, in order to hold the Qi in the spine. Bending any further, the Qi might escape out the base of the spine, instead of staying concentrated in the torso.

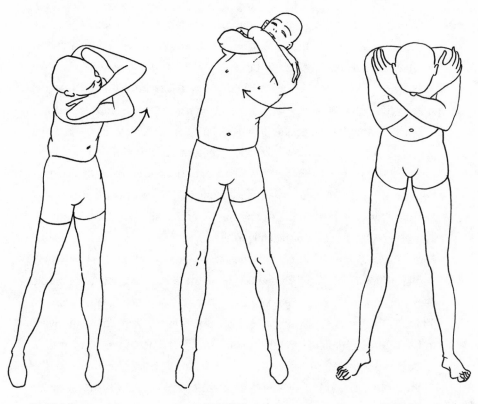

To summarize, turn left, further twisting upward, left, right, left; turn right, twist right, left, right; return to center, stretch all the way up, then down to a forty-five-degree angle. This is one set. Repeat for nine sets. Taking care to breathe with the pulse will bring more Qi into the body and make it easier and less uncomfortable to do this stretch. This stretch is like wringing the water out of a wet towel. By twisting the spine, you are squeezing out the dampness that accumulates in the body. By reaching upward as you twist, you are opening the fascia of the rib cage from the inside out. As you turn, the points along the spine, including the length of the bladder channel, open up. The pressure points that regulate the Five Organs and the Six Hollow Organs are all in the back. Taoist medical theory emphasizes these pressure points as the most direct connection to the organs, each point having its own special purpose. Taoists utilize this kind of stretch to exercise the organs.

These theories differ slightly from mainstream Chinese medicine, but the concept behind them is not too difficult to explain. In Chinese medicine, when applying acupuncture needles, rotating them forward (clockwise) in a point replenishes that point, while twisting them backward (counterclockwise) relieves the point. Though this is generally correct, there is another level of information that has to be considered for complete precision when treating a patient. There are certain specialized acupuncture points that are considered as specifically storing nourishment for the body or dispersing toxins and stagnation. What exactly are you trying to accomplish when you treat these points?

Take for example a patient who has a toothache. Generally, toothache indicates too much heat, principally in the stomach. A doctor may use the Tai Zhong (Liver 3) and Nei Ting Xue (Stomach 44) points to treat the pain. These particular points are dispersal points. The question is, do you twist the needle backward to disperse the excess heat, because that's the specialty of the point? Not necessarily. If your patient is weak from the pain, you might want to twist forward, replenishing the point. You will still be dispersing heat from those points, but with the nourishment found in the clockwise motion of the creative cycle of the Five Elements. A Taoist doctor must learn to recognize what is true replenishment and true dispersal.

In Chinese medicine, the major objective of treatment is to open the channels up so that illness and blockages can be passed through. However, hollowing out the pipe, so to speak, doesn't always take direct force, boring straight through. Sometimes nourishing a related part of the body can be enough to take the pressure off of a blocked organ or channel. You are dispersing by replenishing. For example, constipation is not simply seen as a digestive problem. The lungs and large intestine are viewed together as reciprocal partners. If the lungs' Qi goes down, it can bring the energy of the large intestine down with it. Just simply dispersing by taking a laxative to stimulate the digestion and loosen the bowels would be treating the symptom, not the cause. A doctor of Chinese medicine would not disperse without nourishing the lungs first. Replenishing the lungs up above, the rest can go down by itself.

As you twist your spine, you are using this same theory. By stretching forward, then backward and then forward again on each side of the stretch, you are creating this nourishing and dispersing movement on all the points along the spine. The benefit of this exercise is all in the movement. The point is not to see how far you can stretch, but rather how smoothly you can move. In fact, the second level of this exercise takes the emphasis off of the twisting and focuses almost entirely on the movement of the torso.

The basic stance is the same. Start the twist to the left, but this time instead of continuing the twist all the way up while leading with the elbows, you're going to keep the back flat. Holding tightly on to the shoulders for balance, feel your upper torso moving in the same pattern as before, but gently this time, using your elbows to guide you (Figure 23). It's like a flat figure eight or infinity loop, gaining momentum from around the spinal column. You will feel this centered on the vertebrae between the shoulder blades. While keeping the back flat and the chin tucked, see if you can stretch and lengthen yourself forward, moving forward with your elbows as if you were a fish swimming in the ocean. Concentrate on your breathing pattern and the rolling flow of the movement. This will bring large quantities of Qi into the spine. The more effortlessly you twist, the more Qi you will

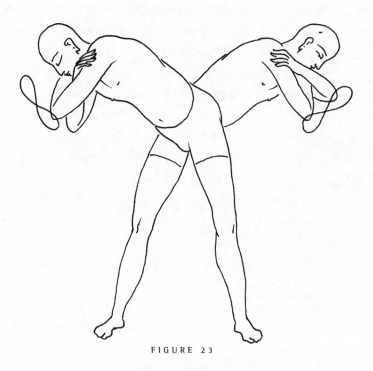

FIGURE 23

be able to absorb into your back. Twist back and forth for about fifteen seconds while turned to the left, then twist right and repeat. Do not stretch up and down facing forward. Just turn back to the left side and continue your rolling motion. Repeat up to nine times on each side, or until your back feels warm.

In the first form of the stretch, you are wringing dampness out of the spine. In the second version, you are also dispersing. However, with a greater emphasis on the movement, you are highlighting replenishment. Why is this? Movement is Yang. By turning your body, you are adjusting the Yang energy in the spine. By adjusting it, you are dispersing the Yang energy outward. But by focusing on the figure-eight motion, you become aware of the fixed point at the center of your spine around which you are pivoting. This is where the nutrition lies, where the generation of new energy is created. With this twist, we are looking for the fertile Yin point from which the moving Yang can grow. *Yang zhong qu Yin*—in the center of Yang moves Yin. Yang energy is being generated up from the core of your spine. This concept of creating body movement around a central pivot point is physically a very simple thing to manage, and yet much of the healing benefit of Qi Gong, as well as its profound mystical insights, can be realized in this motion.

When doing this stretch, you want to feel very comfortable and relaxed, as if you were floating in the Great Void (*taixu*). Let your body easily travel along with the motion, wandering through space. You will be exercising every segment of your spine and all the internal organs. Over time, as you practice this exercise, you will feel surrounded by energy, as if something is holding you, enveloping you in Qi. Your whole body will feel like the still pivot point at the center of the movement. The idea of tangible force rising up from pure, undefined potential is not an impossible abstraction. Through a simple exercise like this, your body can quickly come to a physical understanding of this power. Just relive the experience of being a fish swimming happily in the river. The Taoists have long believed that birds evolved directly from fish. The most recent Western research seems to bear this out. Keep swimming. This stretch works on the parts of our bodies that correspond to the fins of the fish and the wings of the birds. Use those fins enough and one day they will lift you in flight.

BRINGING QI TO THE HANDS

THE FIRST MAJOR operation of 9 Palaces Qi Gong has now been completed. With the ear, neck, and back exercises, the circulation of Qi throughout the nervous system has been stimulated. Next, we have to get the Qi to a place in the body where it can be used like a tool. By exercising the hands and fingers, not only are the terminal points of all the major meridians cleared, the important heart centers in the middle of the palms are opened. As we have said before, the heart is the true mind of the body, with the brain merely carrying out its orders. A crucial goal of the 9 Palaces practice is merging the warmth and will of the heart's energy into each of the other organs. By blending the heart's intent with the organs' functions, you can train your body to become more responsive to your desires. If you want to quickly relax, send healing energy to a sick organ, or recognize cues being sent to you from your body and the outer environment, you must develop this connection. Going back to the analogy of the heart as the emperor and the other organs as the ministers and generals, you can see the importance of creating lines of communication. To run an empire or a body with wisdom, harmony and dialogue must be achieved.

At one level, finger and hand exercises add to general health. The fine capillaries in the hands can easily get blocked. Their circulation needs to be regularly attended to in order to regulate body temperature and therefore strengthen the immune system. Warming the hands accomplishes this, as in warming the ears. Increased circulation in the hands, combined with muscle and joint training of the wrists and fingers, will bring more Qi to these important areas, in the same manner as the neck and spine stretches. Reduced stress on the joints and increased circulation will keep the hands supple, pain-free, and able to withstand the aging process.

As the first hand exercise illustrates, these sorts of strengthening techniques have an even more fundamental purpose. Your hands and fingers, as extensions of your heart and organs, are sensitive tools that interpret and direct the constant flow of Qi circulating throughout the universe. Again, there's nothing magical about this. By opening the microcirculation network

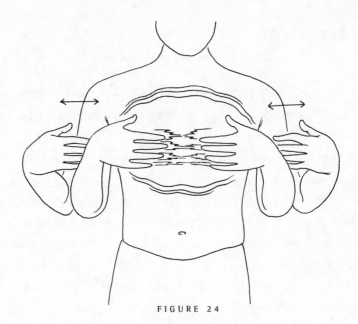

FIGURE 24

in the hands, this exercise stimulates all the circulatory systems in the body: Qi, blood, and nervous systems. Practicing these basic exercises regularly will be enough to reconnect with very natural abilities.

From the shoulders, bring the hands slowly down to face the heart center. They should be held loosely with the fingers gently spread, about two fists' distance away from the chest. Though keeping your eyes shut isn't necessary, this is a nice place to close them and really relax into the exercise. Pull the hands away from each other softly, then feel the magnetism in the fingertips start to build as you bring them together again (Figure 24). Pulling them apart, feel the resistance. Without effort, let their attraction draw them back, almost touching but not quite. It's important to keep the fingers slightly spread and staggered, as if you were about to interlace them. You don't want to move the energy just between the fingertips, but around each entire finger, including the thumbs.

Continue until sensations start to arise in the fingertips and hands. You might feel tingling or an impression of heaviness or thickening. It could also feel as if you are pulling strands of taffy between your fingers. Feel the flowing there. This is the Qi arriving in your hands. If you are having trouble feeling anything, keep your hands closer together. With practice, you will feel a current of energy surrounding your hands, flowing between your fingers. This energy is a combination of Qi, bioelectricity, and magnetic force. This is the energy that binds the cells together. By tuning in to this level of energy, you are consciously building and maintaining your health on a deep cellular level. As you move your hands apart, you will feel this current spreading deep into your body, the Qi of the heart opening and moving as one with the hands. You are creating this connection through your hands and your heart.

The next hand exercise is very ancient. Some consider this one of Lao Zi's original thirteen movements. After allowing the sensation of Qi to come to the hands, hold your hands out in two loose fists in front of the chest (Figure 25). Your hands must be hollow, not clenched, to let the flow of Qi pass through. Starting with the forefingers, cover each finger in turn with the thumb, and then flick the fingers out from under the thumb, nine times for each finger (Figure 26). Work your way down from the forefingers to the pinkies, trying to keep the rest of the fingers curled into the hollow fists at the same time. This takes quite a lot of coordination and strength, especially when you get to the ring fingers and pinkies. Do the best you can, knowing that as you practice, you will be building up this strength. When you have flicked each finger individually nine times, flick all the fingers at once against the thumbs for nine repetitions (Figure 27). The finger flicking should be done gently but explosively, putting your arms and shoulders into it, if you wish. Feel as if you are flicking off all toxins and emotional debris from the tips of your fingers. This exercise stimulates the acupuncture points on the fingertips and hands, opening the meridians and allowing for a steady exchange of Qi into and out of the body.

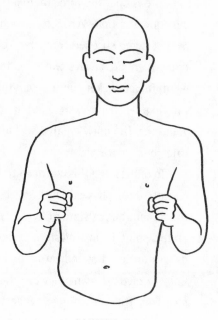

There is a story of a question Confucius posed to Lao Zi: "Why is flicking the fingers considered the

FIGURE 25

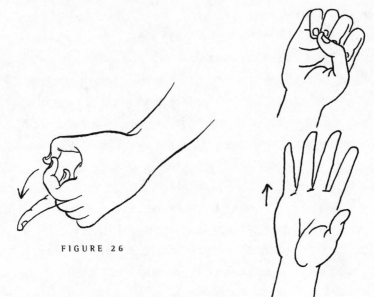

FIGURE 26

FIGURE 27

most important of all the exercises?" Lao Zi replied with a discourse on one-ness. Everything is one. One represents the future. Yin and Yang together are one. Life is one. The force of *Taiji* the Yin Yang symbol, always moves in one direction at a time. Who's to say whether our first cry at birth is from bitter-ness at being stripped from the womb or excitement at beginning our life? While there are always two ways to approach life, with bitterness or excite-ment, finger-flicking unites everything as one. It is said that when practicing the finger-flicking exercise, your true nature, good or bad, is displayed on your face. The unity created within from this practice has the ability to ele-vate your inner self.

To understand this, we need to take a close look at what each finger rep-resents. On a physical level, the condition of the fingers can reveal many things about one's state of health. Western and Chinese medicine both agree on this point. From a Western perspective, symptoms of numbness in the fin-gertips are used as indicators of heart disease and stroke damage. From a Chinese medical point of view, the thumb is a terminal point for the lung meridian. The index finger, while technically the large intestine point, also regulates the lungs. The middle finger begins the Triple Warmer pathways, and the pinkie governs the small intestine and heart. By flicking the fingers, you are clearing these channels.

For a Taoist, the fingers hold a deeper significance. Their magnetism can be developed to resonate with vibrational cues from the environment. For example, a simple but effective training exercise for building vibration sensitivity involves filling a deep bowl with rice, then adding enough water to completely cover the rice by about an inch. Immerse your fingers up to the knuckles and cycle them toward you with a gentle, caressing stroke. Do this for ten minutes every night before you go to sleep. If you can practice for one hundred days without missing a day, your fingers will have a new ability to sense Qi. A healthy or sick plant or a dead animal buried underground will result in different sensations registering on the fingertips as you pass by. This is a very important element in the detection and diagnosis of illness as well. By passing the Qi of the hands along a patient, a skilled Taoist doctor can pinpoint the location and manner of the sickness.

At an even deeper level, each finger resonates with the important people in your life. A sudden sensation felt in a particular finger could indicate changes happening or about to take place in the life of a loved one. Your forefinger represents your mother, the middle finger is for your father, the ring finger stands for your siblings and spouse, and the pinkie depicts your friends. Changes in your own life can be interpreted through your thumbs. The Taoists have thoroughly researched this phenomenon and have outlined many different classes of sensation, each with its separate implications.

This may sound unbelievable, but Dr. Wu has observed this condition time and time again. To relate one story out of many, a patient came to Dr. Wu for treatment. She had severe pain in her forefinger and came to the clinic expecting an acupuncture treatment. Dr. Wu took her aside and told her that to be honest, her condition was not something he could treat medically. She was feeling this pain because there was something wrong with her mother. "How could that be possible?" she replied. Her mother had died many years before. The pain in her finger was her mother's way of reaching out to her from across the levels of the living and the dead. Dr. Wu told his patient to burn her own favorite dress to help her mother, who was cold in the world beyond. After she burned the clothes, her mother would be fine. At first the patient was reluctant to burn her favorite outfit, but after she did, the pain in her finger immediately vanished. There is no way to explain this scientifically. It is part of the wisdom of the Tao.

Finger-flicking not only sensitizes the fingers to pick up on the messages sent out by your friends and family. More important, it helps to relieve any problems that may be affecting them. To see things through the eyes of a Taoist, every part of the body reflects the world around it. There's more than a physical reason why the easiest finger to flick is your forefinger, representing your relationship with your mother. This is the strongest bond a person can have. Just as you are strengthening and straightening your fingers, you are harmonizing and solidifying your relationship with the people who mean the most to you.

The same thing applies to bringing in more luck for yourself. This exercise can help protect you by warning you when trouble is near. One of Dr. Wu's students woke suddenly in the middle of the night with a horrible cramp in her thumb. It was so painful she couldn't fall back to sleep until the early morning. Upon falling asleep, she had a dream in which Dr. Wu was holding her thumb. Just as he was about to tell her how he was going to treat it, her alarm clock rang, again waking her abruptly. All day, her thumb was sore and later that afternoon, she was rear-ended by an uninsured motorist while waiting at a traffic light. As it turned out, she did come to Dr. Wu for treatment and ended up in a better state of health than before the accident. Use the cues picked up by your fingertips to avoid trouble. If you feel an unnatural discomfort in any of your fingers, it should be a signal to you to that danger and disharmony are about. By taking extra time to do plenty of finger flicking, combined with the previous exercise, until the pain subsides, you can avert many potential problems. By merging the energy of your fingers into a whole, you are by extension merging as one with the people in your life, as well as with yourself. By uniting all energies as one within yourself, you will find your other half, that bright, shining star in the heavens above.

FOUR

Returning to the Source

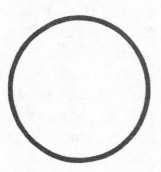

FOR THE TAOIST internal alchemists, the single greatest search along

the path of finding the True Self was aimed at finding the means to reunite

with the other half of one's soul, and so with the rest of the universe. In the

course of their study, numerous insights into the rhythms and patterns of

the body and the universe were discovered. Many were of a concrete phys-

ical nature, making inroads in the fields of medicine, astronomy, chemistry, and meteorology. Others were spiritual and occult. Perhaps the most interesting of their discoveries involve a synthesis of the two. The path toward finding your other half is one of these. Though involving mystical concepts that can only be perceived through esoteric cultivation, this path is firmly rooted in the physical growth of the body.

THE IMMORTAL FETUS

LIKE A SEED SPROUTING into a tall plant, there is a spark of universal energy that grows up within us quite naturally. Taoist Qi Gong seeks to nurture this growth, eliminating obstacles and speeding its maturity. Known in Chinese as *Yuan Ying*, this is the legendary Immortal Fetus. The practice of 9 Palaces Qi Gong is the key to unlock the secrets of this very misunderstood, and very important, concept.

Much has been said of the simplicity and subtle evocativeness of the Chinese language. A single word can act as a portal opening onto a deep, philosophical teaching. *Yuan* literally means "primary." The character is composed of elements that combine to illustrate the concept of the superior human. *Yuan* is also related to another character, similarly pronounced *yuan*, which means "original" "initial," or "first" and is depicted by the image of a mountain spring gushing from the side of a cliff—the source of water. In all, *Yuan* is the Source, the beginning of life.

Ying is a baby or infant, as opposed to a fetus. Herein lies an important distinction. As mentioned in the previous chapter, at the moment of birth, the *hun, shen,* and *po,* or spirit, soul, and animal spirit splits, half entering the newborn baby and the other half remaining as a cosmic particle, or *ling zi,* floating freely through the universe. The inner practice of Taoist Qi Gong attempts to reconnect these two halves into a whole, allowing a whole new level of self-awareness and cosmic insight. This reconnected whole is the *Yuan Ying.* The gestation of the *Yuan Ying* refers to the physical means of bringing the internal and external halves of your being together. It can be understood as a space that can be opened through which your *ling,* or cosmic energy, can flow together. At the same time, it is a living entity with a purpose, the reunification of the self its single goal. As a conduit, the *Yuan Ying* must be developed and maintained. As a growing organism, it must be nurtured and brought into awareness.

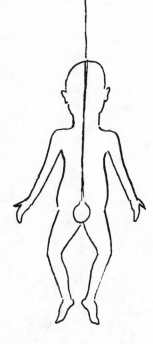

The *Yuan Ying* is present in every person. It lies inside us like a seed waiting to sprout. The 9 Palaces Qi Gong seeks to stimulate and nourish the growth of the *Yuan Ying*. The Taoists believe that there is a strong connection between humans and plants. The human body is commonly visualized as a lotus plant. The parts of the body below the waist are seen as the roots floating under water. The torso is the stem, the leaves the arms, the head the lotus flower, and the brain as the seed pod at the center of the blossom. As the plant strews its seed to perpetuate itself, so too does a person's consciousness shape the events and experiences of his or her life.

The growth of the *Yuan Ying* is also likened to the blossoming of a lotus. At birth, the nascent *Yuan Ying* resides in the lower *dan tian*. In the early years, the *Yuan Ying* takes root in the body and starts to send out a shoot, just as a seed gradually splits open to allow the new sprout to come curling out. At age four, the *Yuan Ying* is strong enough to stand up and start forming the petals of the lotus. Now begins a period of rapid development, where every part of the child's body grows in one coordinated unit—organs, bones, muscles, and the *Yuan Ying*. By nine years of age, the Yuan Ying will have become a nine-petaled lotus.

Besides linking the human body and the lotus, the Taoist sages particularly emphasized the correspondence between humans and trees. The universe is seen as the edge around the circular symbol of Yin and Yang. On this Wheel of Creation, each order of existence has its place. First come humans, then ghosts, then rocks, and so on. The last spot on the circle is reserved for the trees. However, since there is no beginning or ending point in an unbroken circle, trees and human beings are in fact neither separate nor different from each other. Just as trees release oxygen into the air for the benefit of the envi-

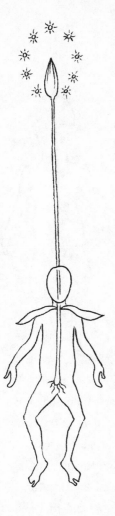

ronment, so do people who practice Qi Gong release positive Qi for the benefit of the rest of the world.

With the proper nourishment, both humans and trees can live long, healthy lives, each making their contributions. What do trees need to grow straight and tall? Water to nourish at the root and sunlight to stimulate photosynthesis for circulating nutrition and generating new cells. With a careful balance of water and sun, the tree bears its fruit. A young tree must be carefully tended so it may safely mature. A sapling needs the perfect balance of sunlight and moisture for its survival. Too much water will lead to infection and rot, while too much fiery heat will burn its tender shoots.

The same holds true for the growth and health of the human body, as well as the *Yuan Ying*. Growth and hormonal balance are directly related to the kidneys and surrounding glands, while proper blood circulation brings oxygen and energy to the cells. After warming the ears, loosening the neck and spine, and bringing the Qi to the hands, the next exercise of 9 Palaces Qi Gong unifies the energy of the kidneys and heart. Balancing the fire of the heart with the water of the kidneys releases a potent new energy that nourishes and strengthens the *Yuan Ying*. This is the mysterious concept of "merging fire and water." Once strengthened, the *Yuan Ying* can continue its upward growth toward bearing its own fruit.

MERGING FIRE AND WATER

"MERGING FIRE AND water" has always been referred to in hushed tones, something unobtainable and impossible to understand, perhaps involving arcane rituals or secret sexual acts. Actually, it's incredibly simple, based on the principles of Chinese and Taoist medicine. The kidneys are con-

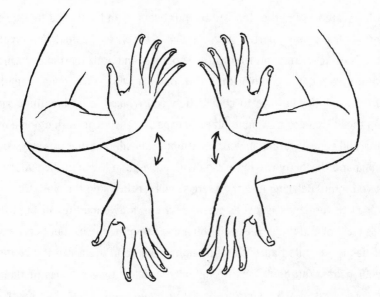

FIGURE 28

sidered the source of water in the body and the heart the source of fire. Since the energy of the heart has outlet points in the centers of the palms, putting them together with the kidneys will bring their energies together. Basically, you want to get the Qi flowing into the hands, then rub them on the lower back, over the kidneys, until the entire area is hot. The increased warmth and circulation will help you to replenish the kidneys' Qi. At a deeper level of understanding, all the nutrients necessary for the healthy growth of the Yuan Ying will be cultivated.

To recap, after finishing the finger-flicking exercises, you have cleared out the terminal points of the meridians in each finger and focused the Qi into the fingertips. Next, you are going to bring the heat from the heart into the center points (*lao gong* points) of the palms. Bring the hands back around so the palms face the chest at heart level. Hold them about two fists' distance away from the body. Start gently shaking your hands at the wrists, keeping everything loose and relaxed, with the palms subtly cupped (Figure 28). The head can be down or up, the eyes open or shut. Gradually increase the speed of the shaking until you are going as fast as you can, your hands a blur.

Take care to keep the standard of four beats to an inhale and four beats to an exhale breathing pattern as you shake. It's very easy to hold your breath with this exercise. This can lead to the shoulders and arms tensing up, which is not only tiring, but can block the flow of Qi, leaving you sore and breathless. As usual, if you have to choose between relaxed, even breathing and doing the exercise to maximum physical capacity, always go with doing a little less and concentrating on your breathing. You will find that this way, your stamina and flexibility will more rapidly improve than if you pushed yourself past your limit. Relaxing into the exercise will let the Qi do the work for you.

Shake your hands as fast as possible for one to two minutes, or until the hands feel hot and tingly. Feel as if you are fanning the fire in your heart with your hands, until its flames shoot straight from your chest into the centers of your palms. You don't have to actually visualize fiery tongues of flame. Just concentrate on transferring heat into your palms from your heart in whatever way works for you. The harder you concentrate on this, the quicker your hands will heat up. Otherwise, you might be shaking your hands for quite a while before you feel any change. You are not necessarily going to feel any strong sensations when you first start practicing this exercise, but firmly concentrating on the connection between the heart center and the centers of the palms will speed up your results. Another added benefit of setting your attention between heart and hands is that it will allow the warm Qi to evenly spread not only into the palms, but open out through the chest cavity and arms as well.

Leaning forward very slightly from the waist can make it easier to shake your hands faster and for a longer time without tiring. Letting gravity hold you up in this manner takes stress off the chest, opening the rib cage. Shaking the hands in this position optimizes the blood flow throughout the body, especially to and from the heart. By drawing excess tension out from the chest, where it is so often stored, the internal organs can relax. The motion of the shoulders and arms that comes along with shaking your wrists also rapidly disperses blockages in the chest as well. You might feel this pent-up energy flowing across the chest, down the arms, then filling the hands as you concentrate on the connection between the centers of the palms and the heart. Regular practice balances the circulation throughout the upper body.

By shaking the excess energy of the heart into the hands, you ease the duties of our hardest-working muscle. In effect, you are training your body to pick up the slack for your heart, saving it from overwork.

This is an excellent exercise for sore wrists. If you spend all day at the typewriter or have a sports injury, warming and loosening your wrists in this manner will give you fast relief. Also, the Taoists believe that this exercise has the ability to calm a troubled heart, or even erase unhappy memories left over from childhood. One of Dr. Wu's students is a well-known Chinese medical doctor who has used this exercise to great effect with his patients. Frequently, if patients come to him in the middle of a severe panic attack, he will practice hand-shaking with them for ten or fifteen minutes in lieu of giving them acupuncture, and they will calm themselves and begin to breathe normally again. It's a very useful technique for managing emotional stress. It efficiently releases tension and traumatic experiences.

This might seem like a simple if slightly strenuous exercise. Don't underestimate its physical and psychosomatic effects. You are redistributing Qi, blood circulation, and nerve impulses throughout the entire upper body. The lungs, heart, liver, and brain are all cleansed by this total circulation enhancer. If you recognize the connection between emotional states and deeply entrenched tension trapped in the organs, it's easy to understand how releasing this rigidity can bring emotional as well as physical release.

Once your hands are thoroughly heated, quickly stop and fold your hands into light fists, as if to grab onto all the Qi you have just generated. Then lean over at the waist at no more than a forty-five-degree angle, place your hot palms over your kidneys (the back of the waist), and start rubbing vigorously up and down (Figure 29). Transfer the heat in your hands and heart through your skin and muscle into your kidneys. Keep rubbing until the entire area is very hot. Again, this is a spot where it is particularly easy to hold your breath. This very vigorous exercise works out your shoulders and arms as much as it heats your kidneys. Make every effort to keep your breath as light and regular as you can. It will give you the stamina you will need to fully stimulate your circulation in this crucial spot.

Some people have a tendency to look down at their feet when rubbing their kidneys. This will work against them by overarching the back, causing

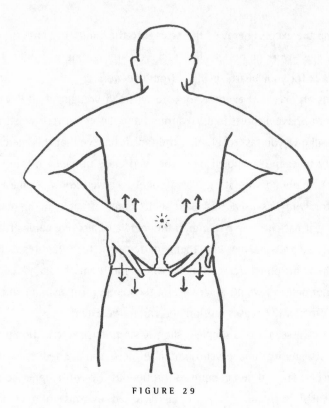

FIGURE 29

stress on the shoulders and making it difficult to breathe properly. Keep your chin tucked in, eyes looking forward, in order to keep your spine perfectly straight and your chest and shoulders relaxed. You want to lean forward slightly to give your shoulders a good range of motion as you rub. Also, lean-ing forward allows all the organs to hang freely, taking pressure off the rib cage and upper chest, which could tense up otherwise. However, you don't want to lean forward more than forty-five degrees. Bending over too far at the waist will cause the Qi to "slide" off the spine, instead of pooling at the lower back over the kidneys.

Ideally, rub the kidneys vigorously at least one hundred times for the greatest healing effect. Rubbing your palms on bare skin is best, though not absolutely necessary. The point is to create the maximum amount of friction and heat. Keep concentrating on the connection between the heart and the centers of the palms, feeling it flow like liquid fire into the kidneys. This might create a powerful sensation, as if receiving an electric jolt. This is a common experience when starting to practice Qi Gong. Remember that you are putting large amounts of bioelectric energy into your body. All the warm-up exercises of 9 Palaces Qi Gong help train the body to absorb greater quantities of Qi. With time, you will become literally more "grounded," and these effects will gradually subside. In the meantime, try to keep your balance and breath and keep on rubbing.

Rubbing the kidneys, after shaking the hands energetically, replenishes the kidneys' *jing,* or essence. This aids a wide variety of kidney diseases, including kidney stones, infections, and various degrees of renal toxicity. From a Chinese medical perspective, nourishing the kidneys in this manner also is beneficial for the organs related to the kidneys. Urogenital disorders, lower back pain, premature ejaculation, impotence, and other, particularly male, fertility problems can all be addressed by strengthening kidney essence.

It's crucial to make the hands hot before beginning to rub the kidneys. Though you can practice the hand-shaking exercise independently of rubbing the kidneys, do not start the kidney-rubbing unless you have shaken your hands until they are hot. To achieve the maximum benefit from this exercise, the heart's essence must be aroused and concentrated into the *lao gong* points in the palms. In order for the heart and kidneys to communicate, for fire and water to merge, they must first "see" each other. If you can picture the important points of the body as each having their own set of eyes that can make contact with one another, just as two lovers gaze into each other's eyes, you are very close to the Taoist understanding of communication.

This is the first of many exercises in 9 Palaces Qi Gong where the nourishing power of the heart is fused with the energy of the other organs in order to uplift and lighten their functions. Taoist esoteric medicine focuses on getting the total body's systems to work together in a cooperative manner. The "Merging Fire and Water" exercise is a good illustration of this concept. The kidneys are the embodiment of the water element. This makes practical sense, considering that the natural product of the kidneys is urine. All the negative implications of water—coldness, being waterlogged—can be cleared up by applying a little fire, the element represented by the heart. Water, on the other hand, is the perfect way to quench an out of control blaze. All of water's negative qualities now come in quite handy. Water and fire, though on the surface antithetical to each other, actually can help each other a great deal—if they "agree to agree." This is true communication. Water is working together with fire, two friends at a higher level of mutual understanding.

To take this a step further, not only the kidneys and heart are connecting in this exercise. If a man is excessively nervous, a Taoist doctor will diagnose his problem as stemming from a weak liver. He will treat the patient by nourishing his liver. The liver is the wood element. The kidneys are water. Water feeds wood. The positive, life-sustaining characteristics of water have as important a use as its negative, controlling aspects. Rubbing the kidneys increases and enhances the function of the liver like water helps a plant to grow.

Along with the liver, the lungs are also brought into play by kidney rubbing. Besides the obvious fact that the harder you rub your kidneys, the more you exercise every part of your chest, Five Elements theory is subtly at work. Though the lungs represent the metal element and metal officially nourishes water, the reasoning behind this can get rather obscure. It starts to make more sense when one learns that the Taoists also conceptualize the lungs as white clouds. Clouds produce rain. What could be more natural, or auspicious? Just as heart fire clears up dampness in the kidneys, it can revitalize chill and stagnation in the lungs. Again, rubbing the kidneys brings it all home.

Liver, lungs, heart, kidneys: all of these organs are fused together at the point directly opposite the navel by rubbing the back. This point is known as the *Ming Men*—the Gates of Life. The *Ming Men* is often referred to as being of water. This is no ordinary water, as relates to the kidneys. It's better to think of it as the water one finds in the Fountain of Youth, for the *Ming Men* is also the seat of *jing*, or vital essence. Specifically, this is the prenatal *jing*, the part of your essence that belongs to your other half in the heavenly realm. You can think of the *Ming Men* as the physical anchor point of your other half. By rubbing the kidneys, you are not only promoting fertility and longevity, you are enhancing your attachment to your other half's portion of *hun* (soul), *shen* (spirit), and *po* (animal spirit). When we recognize that according to Taoist inner alchemy the *hun* resides in the liver, the *shen* in the heart, the *po* in the lungs, and the water that unites them all in the kidneys, a true marvel is revealed. We have come full circle, back to the growth of the *Yuan Ying*.

Here is the singular medicine for the physical as well as the spiritual self. It's a perfectly elegant demonstration of how nourishing the body physically simultaneously nourishes it on the most subtle energetic plane. As a person places him or herself as the balance point between the movements of Heaven and Earth, the spark that feeds his or her continued growth is struck. Merging fire and water is no different than merging Heaven and Earth, which is no different than simply increasing the health of your kidneys by rubbing them until they are hot.

After being vitalized by this nourishment, the Yuan Ying continues its upward climb. When upon birth the *hun*, *shen*, and *po* split in two, half enters the human infant, or *ren ying*, through the navel and descends to take root in the lower *dan tian*. It grows from the lower *dan tian* to the middle *dan* and then to the upper *dan*. From there, it flows down to the Ming Men point, that link to the moment of birth—and separation—then directly back through to the navel. As the circuit completes, the Ren and Du channels that circle the body are fully activated. Like the point on the circle that is both its beginning and ending mark, the *Yuan Ying* becomes ready to emerge from the body after a cycle that returns it to the place that holds the memory of birth. At this stage, the body is suffused and surrounded by a halo of white light. This is the sign that the *Yuan Ying* has been released from the body. It is now free to travel throughout every dimension of the universe, two halves united as one, free and without limits. The Human Tree has progressed to the next stage—the Dragon Tree.

In this idea, the Taoist representation of the universe as the unbroken circle of Tai Chi is taken one step further. Since every point in this circle flows together with the next, the Taoist sages consider there is actually very little separation between the different orders of creation. In our travels before and after this life as a cosmic particle, we pass through and encounter every type of existence—animal and mineral, plant and pure energy. Our *ling* experiences it all. When we learn to release our *Yuan Ying* from the body, it passes through all solid objects, beyond every dimension of space and time to the Heavenly Realms, searching ceaselessly until it finds and unites with our other half, known as the *mi ying,* or "secret infant." Rejoining with our *ling* Qi, we can achieve a level of wisdom that stays with us, aiding the decisions we make in our lives and showing us the way toward new forms of cultivation and service. Ultimately we come to recognize our true purpose in the cosmic scheme. This is the wisdom of the Dragon and each one of us has it deep within us, waiting to be brought out.

Now the image of the Tai Chi symbol becomes clear. The circle is the universe. The spark of Yin that grows within the field of Yang reaching heavenward is the *Yuan Ying.* It is the humble seed that shoots upward, uniting physical existence with cosmic awareness. The point of Yang within the Yin is what we give back to the world from our journey to our other half—the Human Tree and the Dragon Tree. As the tall trees touch the sky with their prayers, so too do the dragons with their flight. So too do we with the practice of Qi Gong. Everything that reaches up to heaven is a tree. An ancient Taoist proverb states *Tai yang yi huo long, ren shi yi jing ling*: "The Sun is the Fire Dragon, Humankind is the essential energy of the cosmos." As the highest form of tree, we may release our prayers anywhere we may be. As the tree produces oxygen, we produce healing light—the light of the Yuan Ying released. The practice of Qi Gong while standing in front of a tree and facing the sun is simply a ritual designed to embody this important trinity—Human Tree, Fire Dragon, and Yuan Ying, the process of bringing blessings, wisdom and mercy to the world.

CLAIMING YOUR POSTNATAL QI

THE NAVEL IS the beginning point of your earthly life; the point through which your earthly portion of *hun, shen,* and *po* is distributed, the entry point of your postnatal *jing.* While rubbing the kidneys addresses prenatal essence, the next exercise of the 9 Palaces form stakes a firm claim to the portion of you that you came into this world with.

After having rubbed the kidneys over the *Ming Men* point until they are hot, bring the hands back up to heart level. With the forearms raised slightly higher than parallel with the ground, press together the thumb, fore-

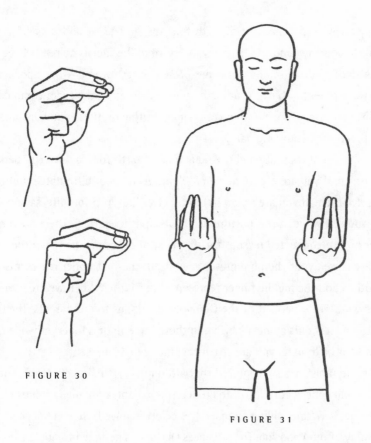

FIGURE 30

FIGURE 31

finger, and middle finger of each hand (Figure 30). With the hands in this mudra, close your eyes and count down each number that forms the date of your birth, year, month, and day, in that order, nine times in a row (Figure 31). For example, if you were born on October 17, 1952, you would repeat "one—nine—five— two—one—zero—one—seven" nine times. Speak these numbers silently in your mind. If you know the exact time of your birth, include the numbers that make up the hour and minutes as well. Only include birth time numbers if you are positive of their accuracy. If not, you are better off leaving them out than guessing.

The person you were born into this world as was created by Heaven and Earth. The moment you were born, the best part of you was born—what is most truly you. Your birth was perfectly timed, generated by that unique blend of Yin and Yang that was specially meant for you. Remember that it's only at the exact moment of birth that the *hun, shen,* and *po* split in two, half to your *ren ying* and half to your *mi ying.* The Taoists do not believe that the spirit, soul, or animal spirit are present in the womb—they appear only at the moment of birth. Your birth numbers represent the exact combination of Yin and Yang forces within you. Concentrating on these numbers puts you in touch with your Original Qi.

The numbers that comprise your time of birth form a powerful personal talisman. If you are experiencing problems, recite your birth date numbers to resolve them. If you are trying to bring better luck into your life, saying them to yourself while in this posture will have a positive effect. There are a number of interconnected reasons for this. First of all, as mentioned in the previous chapter, your thumb represents yourself, the first finger represents your mother, and the middle finger represents your father. When we are born into the world, fifty percent of the Qi involved belongs to our parents. The other 50 percent is ours alone. By bringing these three fingers together while reciting your birth date, you are strengthening your 50 percent.

The Taoist sages recognized that although certain aspects of life, such as the family one is born into, are predetermined, there are many things we can change. If we are willing to make the effort involved, we can lay claim to a destiny of our choosing. The 9 Palaces Qi Gong is designed to guide the practitioner back to the place in his or her timeline before cause and effect stepped in to alter its course.

The big picture for a Taoist is that life is eternal. Life will never disappear or become extinguished. The physical realm will never diminish. Reincarnation is accepted as fact. Where you end up in the Six Realms of material existence will vary. This time you are human, next time maybe something else. The circumstances of cause and effect will determine the outcome for the next rotation. The wheel of death operates on the same arc as a leaf. A leaf is born of energy traveling up from the roots of a tree. It returns the favor by absorbing the sun's rays and releasing oxygen. Gradually the leaf dies and flutters to the ground, absorbed into the Earth to begin the nutritive cycle anew.

This earthly life is only one stopping point on a long journey across many planes. According to Taoist mystical lore, we start out as a single cosmic particle, generated from the flow of the Milky Way, known in Chinese as the Silver River. The symbol of the birth of the universe is the right-facing swastika. We spin along with the multitude of galaxies in this clockwise curve. Eventually, tendencies and forces come into play. We alight in one of the Six Realms: Hell, Heaven, Plant, Animal, Ghost, or Human. Like the leaf, we exist for our allotted span and then break down again into *ling* Qi.

In the cycle of death and rebirth, our cosmic selves have many opportunities to experience life in each of these realms. Based on our prior choices and actions, we come back again, perhaps in the same realm but in a different form, or perhaps in another realm. Often we bring traces of our past existences with us into our latest incarnation. A famous actress once came to Dr. Wu to have her fortune told. Among other things, he told her that she had been a fox in another life. She was quite curious about this, having already been told the same thing by other fortunetellers. Dr. Wu told her he would be happy to continue their discussion over dinner. He ordered a number of different dishes to be brought out all at once. She went straight for the chicken. She didn't touch anything else on the table. She was enjoying it so much she even chewed on the bones. She ate very fast, as if hiding, not wanting anyone to see her. After the meal, she again asked Dr. Wu about her past life. "You were a fox all right," he told her. "What else could you have been, the way you ate that chicken?" She asked him how it could be possible, if he hadn't even read her Qi. He told her it didn't matter. No investigation was needed. Through someone's behavior, acts, and movements, not to mention their diets, you can tell what they once were.

After death, a spirit circles the Earth as *ling* Qi, rewarding those who helped it and exacting revenge on its enemies. Many times, a sudden, unexplained accident or cash windfall can be traced to a departed soul paying you back for all the things it couldn't in life. Once the *ling* particle passes through the Six Realms, tying up the loose ends from its last life, it is reborn. This rebirth happens every second of time. The number of births in each second is exactly 99,999. These are not only human births. This figure also includes animals, plants, and flowers.

The Taoist universe is supremely intelligent. There is a reason for everything. Nothing is without timing or purpose, whether it's a leaf falling or an elevator door opening. All these things are as they should be. As such, there's also a special reason for being born into your particular group. Each group of 99,999 is predetermined by vast cosmic forces and shares a common purpose. Each group has its own sex as well. Every member of a group of 99,999 will be either male or female. This is predetermined by the heavens, arranged by the Nine Levels of Clear Light.

All beings in a group come into this world at the same moment and are destined to depart the Earth Realm together to continue their travels. Although they are born at the same time, they may die at different times. This is determined by the actions of each individual. If they kill another, their longevity will be decreased. If they steal, cheat, or wrong another, their life span will be shortened. Don't think that only people can do harm to others. A tree can fall on a living creature, killing it. A fungus can infect a tree. An animal can violently attack. As we all live in the Realm of Earth, we all have something to do with killing, either directly or indirectly, one way or another. This is the standard measure of existence on this planet. We each came here due to circumstances from past lives. The group we are born into, our sex, our family, our level of knowledge, problems, fortune, and obstacles—all are predetermined.

Should we timidly accept this prearrangement and go along about our lives unconsciously? How do we change what has been decreed? Cultivate the self. Cultivate yourself to understand the forces at work around you. Develop the affections and the noble emotions. Strengthen your connection to the part of you that has always existed beyond this realm. Not only is the practice of Qi Gong beneficial to yourself, it helps the other members of your group. Any group members that have died before it was time due to an abundance of sin are forced to wait for the rest of the group. They exist in a limbo known as "lonely souls." In this state, they are extremely vulnerable. They may be preyed upon by other, stronger forces that have the power to completely erase their *ling* Qi. They also can be a threat. They might attempt to attach themselves to living members of their group, applying pressure upon them to do wrong in order to hurry them up.

In the monastery, the master would take sixty-four days to fully explain the intricacies of these group dynamics. From a Taoist perspective, even if you do good in your life, bad things still can happen. The good deeds you do will help change your fate to a certain extent, but the practice of Qi Gong has the power to make changes on a deeper level. It pushes sickness and evil away by developing a positive force that operates on karmic as well as physical and energetic levels. By shoring up your Original Qi, negativity finds less of a footing. Only through practice can one experience the full implications of this. It is as much a physical awareness as a philosophical truth. Without Qi Gong, there is no Taoist tradition. Without Qi, there is no existence.

These are the deep objectives behind reciting your birth numbers while using the three-fingered mudra. As you silently repeat them nine times, hold the awareness of their far-reaching ability to affect your life. It will connect you with your destiny. You want to hold your fingers in place until they feel very strong, as if they are made of steel. In the Shaolin temple, this posture is used to develop power as part of Eagle Claw and Iron Claw martial arts training. The Taoists use this training to generate powerful healing energy in the fingertips.

Use your mind to focus the energy into the fingertips. By concentrating your complete attention on the point where the fingers unite, you are focusing power from the mind. Associating your birth date with this posture focuses emotional energy from the Heart Center. The force of your mental and emotional energy combined is the expression of your ethical nature. In this state of concentration, all the good you have done wells up from deep within. It causes a very special Qi to arrive in the fingertips. This Qi is unique. It has been energized by the ethical accumulation of your heart and mind. Daily practice of this posture brings your Righteous Qi into your hands, turning them, in time, into potent healing tools.

Once you build up the Qi in your thumb and first and middle fingers, you are going to use them to again nourish the kidneys. As soon as you feel the steely sensation, bend over at the waist and fit the thumb and first and second fingers in the indentations around the kneecap in a claw-like gesture (Figures 32 and 33). Make sure your back is perfectly flat and your knees are locked (Figure 34). Looking straight ahead rather than down at your hands will help keep your back in position. Lightly tucking the chin into the neck will further decrease any strain on the spine. You want to keep the legs rigid to loosen and isolate the tissue covering the kneecap. This allows your fin-

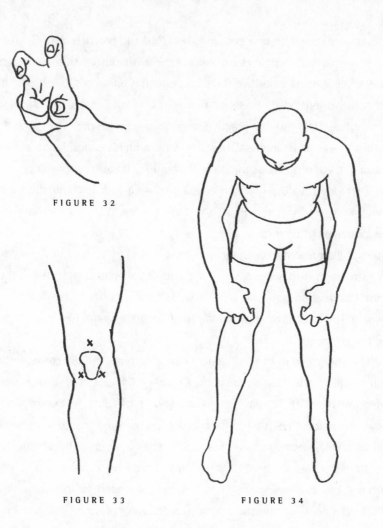

FIGURE 32

FIGURE 33

FIGURE 34

gers to better find their mark. Feel the Qi entering these three points as you grip them firmly and start rotating. You want to rotate the kneecaps until they feel as if the Qi inside them has taken on a circular motion of its own. Circle both kneecaps at once in a clockwise direction. Remember that clockwise is considered as if you are the face of the clock. In other words, if you consider your clockwise rotation as beginning from the top of the circle, you would be rotating from right to left and around, back up to the top. This takes a little coordination, but besides stimulating the basic circulation of Qi to knees and kidneys, the clockwise motion specifically tonifies and nourishes them as well. Generally speaking, clockwise movements replenish, while counterclockwise motions disperse. This is the disadvantage to rotating the knees outward or haphazardly rotating them one way, then another. Rotating the knees outward will only aid in improving the circulation around your knees, while rotating in both directions at the same Qi Gong session would be detrimental, as you would be canceling out your results. Try your best to work your coordination up to the point where you rub the knees only clockwise. You will gain the greatest benefit this way.

While we're on the subject of the knees, a moment should be taken to discuss a very subtle yet important aspect of internal Qi circulation. The joints act as receptacles for Qi within the body. Actually, to be more specific, the joints are not only storage receptacles for Qi, but springboards for releasing Qi outward from and throughout the body. Think of how a cat rears back on its haunches before it springs forward or how a bird presses down from its knees before it takes off in flight. If you practice martial arts, your internal force is coming out not from your muscle strength but from the momentum generated as the Qi bounces out of the joints. A superior martial artist barely needs to make any motions with his body to stop his opponent. The force of the Qi being expelled from subtly releasing his joints will be enough. In fact, in the monastery, the monks' martial arts ability was judged and graded before they even started their form, just by virtue of their posture and state of relaxed but ready tension in their arms, legs, and waist.

This is why so much care is taken in loosening and increasing the circulation in the joints. Your Qi Gong practice will be greatly enhanced if you always keep your knees and elbows slightly bent and relaxed. Also keep all motions involving arms, legs, waist, and shoulders light and flexible. To increase their relaxation, remember the principle of kong, or emptiness. A glass has to be empty to fill it with fresh water. Just so, feel the hollow and ready receptivity in your joints as your motions fill them with Qi. The gentle movements of the 9 Palaces Qi Gong warm-ups will increase the soft, flowing feeling that draws in maximum Qi, and the self-massage techniques will increase circulation, unblocking clogs that could hinder your sensation of emptiness, necessary for greatest Qi storage.

The one difference between bringing Qi to the joints and to the organs is that the joints are temporary storage points, like locks in a canal regulating the level and flow of water. As you will see further along in the following chapters, bringing Qi to the organs in 9 Palaces Qi Gong cleanses and stores Qi for future use. Next time you take a walk, try putting a little spring in your step by being aware of the Qi in your joints. You will definitely find yourself more graceful and lighter on your feet.

Taoist medicine has given the three points around the kneecap colorful names that indicate the importance of this area for longevity. The two points along the bottom are the "Tiger's Eyes" and the upper point is the "Crest of the Crane." Of course, cranes relate to immortality and tigers relate to strength and sexual vigor. With this kneecap massage, you are enhancing the function of the kidneys. Weak, rickety knees and difficulty lifting your feet off the ground generally indicate kidney depletion. Taoist doctors very often will treat kidney problems by treating the kneecaps. While rubbing the kidneys directly helps to replenish their *jing*, or essence, treating the kneecaps also helps to clear up many symptoms related to long-term endocrine imbalance. The aging process usually results in a slowdown in hormone production. Sexual function and fertility deteriorate. Although its influence is very gradual, frequent knee massage can help reverse these signs of age. With time, sexual and reproductive capability are enhanced. Sperm motility is improved, as well as female fertility. Though it might take a while to see results, the changes made using this technique take root at a deep level and can make a permanent positive impact on your health. Generally, it should take about one month of knee massage practice, rotating the kneecaps at least twenty-seven times every day, to notice a difference. Of course, the more you rotate them, the more beneficial it is. Circling the kneecaps one hundred to two hundred times in one session will really make the Qi surge up through your body. Try it and see.

By keeping the back flat and the legs locked when bending over to rotate the kneecaps, the kidney meridian channels that run down the legs are straightened and elongated. In this posture, you will over time feel the Qi coursing between the kidneys and the legs, sometimes even connecting with the Qi from the heart. Remember that the Qi tends to pool in the joints. By rotating the kneecaps, you are helping these important switching points to release their energy to the entire body.

The Taoists describe this three-fingered grip as resembling an eagle's talons as it grasps its prey. It's very instructive to study pictures and videos of eagles catching salmon out of the water. Especially in slow motion, the strength and minute control of their claws are an inspiration. Holding the image of the eagle's talons in mind while rotating the kneecaps can help put more healing force into your practice.

The 9 Palaces kneecap rotation should be done with three fingers when at all possible. People who have difficulty using three fingers can use all five or just the palms to circle. However, the results won't be as dramatic. The important points to remember are fitting the fingers into the three indentations around the kneecap and making sure that as you rotate, you are moving the tissue over the kneecap (the patella) along with the fingers. If it's difficult to do the exercise standing, or if you want to practice an extra amount to treat a particular health condition, it's all right to sit down and start circling. As with the rest of 9 Palaces Qi Gong, it's better to do only what is most comfortable for your level of health and ability while maintaining the proper breathing pattern. There's no way to do these exercises "wrong." As you practice, you will notice steady improvement, no matter what level you are on.

FIVE

The Medicine of Heaven and Earth

CROSSING THE BRIDGE

BY RUBBING THE kidneys and rotating the kneecaps, the nourishing kidney essence and the stimulating energy of the heart are brought together, each one helping the other. Both halves of the *hun, shen,* and *po,* prenatal and postnatal, are contacted. The next step is returning body and mind to the moment before these two halves split off. The goal of the next exercise of 9 Palaces Qi Gong is to bring the practitioner back to that origin point. It's the culmination of all the exercises that have come before it. As with the growth of the Yuan Ying, to start the next leg of the journey, you have to come full circle, back to where you first began. Through the practice of 9 Palaces Qi Gong, your body will come to understand the most profound teachings of Taoism. Again, you learn with a simple practice that in its simplicity connects with deep psychosomatic triggers in the brain.

After the energy in the kneecaps seems to be revolving on its own, stand straight again, lifting the arms up in front of the chest in a rounded posture, as if you were holding a large barrel. The palms are facing the chest and should be held roughly a foot away from the body. Closing the eyes lightly, collect your breathing until it returns to a smooth four beats per inhale/four beats per exhale. As you relax, think back to your earliest happy childhood memories. Place them vividly in your mind until the years melt away and you're there again, a little child running, laughing, and playing. If you feel blocked, as if the memories won't come, don't be discouraged. Even if you only have one small, shadowy recollection, latch onto it. Often we attempt to remember things visually, while as a child we may have imprinted our reactions to the environment through smell, touch, or taste.

As you start going back to that early moment, start rocking forward and backward, using the whole foot as you sway. As you come forward, try to come up as far as you can on the balls of your feet (Figure 35). Going backward, lift your feet all the way, until you are poised on the edges of the heels (Figure 36). Keep your balance with the roundness of your arms. Tuck your chin in and use the muscles on your back and abdomen for support. Flat, closed shoes or bare feet are a must here.

The further you can rock your body forward and back, the more deeply held internal tension you can release. Holding a happy memory in your mind, or alternately, an ideal image of yourself in a radiant state of perfection, is integral to the physical movement. It will help connect your body, mind, and heart, adding to the sense of release. Surprisingly, it can also make it easier to keep your balance as you sway. If it becomes difficult to keep the visualization because you feel you might fall over backward, practice your swaying

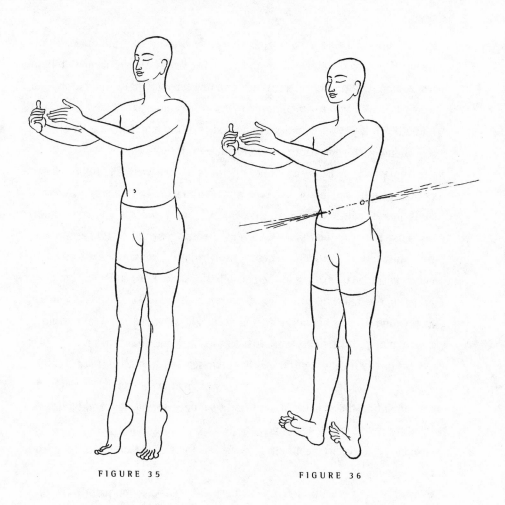

FIGURE 35   FIGURE 36

standing with your back to a wall. The perfect distance is two and a half to three feet away. Another possibility is to stand with a bed or sofa nearby. It's perfectly all right if you want to put less arc into it when you are just starting out. Give yourself whatever you need to feel free to sway for the next few minutes.

The Chinese name for this exercise is *Guo Qiao*, or "Crossing the Bridge." On the edges of your feet, it's as if you are standing at the brink of a narrow rope bridge stretched far across a mountain pass. As you walk across, you feel the swing of the bridge all around you, down and back, down and back. With this movement, you balance the Yin and Yang within your body. Coming forward is Yang, going backward is Yin. As you sway, become aware of the circuit connecting your navel and the *Ming Men* point. Your navel is Yin within the forward momentum of Yang. The *Ming Men* is Yang potential developing within Yin. Let this direct channel linking what came before you were born with what will come help you to free yourself of all things that might block you. Your conscious mind stands in the middle of the movement of Yin and Yang. Sink yourself into its motion to unite with it.

The whole year is regulated by the four seasons. All life on Earth responds to the passing of cold to warmth, from scarcity to plenty. Just as the birds migrate south in the fall, our planet changes its activity in response to the seasons of the solar system. Using the wisdom of the *I Ching* as a guide, the Taoist sages have spent generations calculating the seasons of the heavenly bodies, the galaxies, and the constellations, each one shifting, changing, affecting one another. For example, currently, there will be a steady increase in flooding across the world. This is because right now our solar system is in the middle of its fall season. Just as the Earth has four seasons, the solar system has four seasons. The sun has four seasons. The Milky Way has four seasons. Our bodies have four seasons. By practicing Crossing the Bridge you are regulating the seasons of your body, summer, spring, fall, and winter. At its root are the movements and changes expressed by the *I Ching*. All Taoist cosmology, all Taoist health treatments, all Taoist philosophy are based on this swaying.

This practice will bring you way back. Most people who practice it for a short period of time begin remembering childhood events they haven't thought of since they first happened. There's no telling how far back this gentle, natural sensation of swaying will take you. Students of Dr. Wu have reported experiences ranging from suddenly recalling long-forgotten toys and games to reliving the moment of birth, the sensations of the womb, or the instant of conception. When we approached Dr. Wu on this subject, wondering just how far back this practice could take us, he told us it was endless. It could go as far back as the creation of the universe.

On a more prosaic level, this is a wonderful exercise for strengthening the lower back and abdominal muscles. To keep your balance, as you rise up on your heels, dig down into them with a smooth contraction of the back muscles from the shoulders down to the legs. Then imagine yourself being pulled forward on a line extending from the *Ming Men* out through the navel. You will feel your abdominal walls crunching as you sway. Don't hold your breath. Let your joyful memories help your breathing stay calm and even. Continue rocking until your waist is warm and your feet are very hot. This takes an average of five to ten minutes.

In the past, Dr. Wu hesitated to show this practice to his patients for fear that they might topple over backward and hurt themselves. It's okay to stumble around a bit as you sway. Just make sure you are either near a wall or tree, or at the very least are practicing in an uncluttered area with nothing around that you could trip on or hit yourself against. That old saw about an ounce of prevention definitely applies here.

As you regulate yourself by swaying, heavy toxins in the body are being shaken down toward the feet. One of the indicators that you have practiced Crossing the Bridge long enough is that your feet should be warm, even hot. Just as the ear exercises treat the entire body, due to their many corresponding stimulation points, the swaying practice works the entire body through the feet. Taoist medicine is complementary. In order to treat one part of the body, the Taoist doctor often won't treat it directly. Instead, the related part will be treated, in order to achieve a balance of energy. This might make the treatment take longer to have noticeable results, but the effects will have greater permanence. A Taoist doctor will balance the kidneys to subdue an overstimulated heart. Basically, a Taoist health regimen works with Yin and Yang, making sure there is harmony. So if there's a problem with your head, a Taoist doctor will treat your feet. In this context, there are enormous health benefits to be had from enhancing the circulation in the feet. By swaying your body back and forth, you are giving yourself a total foot stretch and massage.

After spending enough time rocking to feel warmth in the stomach muscles and feet, a sensation of fullness, roundness, and calm may arise. As mentioned above, a circuit of energy between Yin and Yang forces within the body has been generated. If one can accept that potential for dynamic change as well as for repression and anxiety are both continually at play within the confines of the physical body, we can start to understand how simple movements, based on an understanding of the meridians, can rally these forces, and synthesize and harmonize them. This is a critical juncture in the practice of 9 Palaces Qi Gong. Crossing the Bridge is the first stage toward forging a field of energy around the body that will be a secure catalyst for change on a deep internal level. This crucial cocoon of vital energy will be returned to and further strengthened in the course of the 9 Palaces form. A Taoist adage states, *Hui ying wang yi ji*: "Returning to infancy, one forgets even the self." As you sway, you have no cares, no troubles, no happiness. With this practice, you can easily achieve a sense of tranquility, transparent as a still lake. Another saying declares, *Ren zhi qu xin ben shen.* Loosely translated, this means, "In returning to one's original nature, sanctity is found." Practicing this primal movement, you can reconnect with the innocent purity of your inner child. Reawakening youthful wonder, the best qualities of your heart will be free to come out from the dark corners they hid within for so long. Taoist Qi Gong has recognized for thousands of years how easy it is to lose this precious spark, and how simple it is to regain.

TAOIST MASSAGE

CROSSING THE BRIDGE is a wonderful, all-purpose massage for the feet, and by extension for many other parts of the body, due to the numerous critical pressure points on the soles. There is a long history of healing massage in Taoist tradition, fine-tuned for health and spiritual aid. There are detailed techniques of rubbing, hitting the body with lengths of different types of wood for different illnesses, and visualizations for the practitioner as well as the patient. All in all, the main purpose of Taoist massage is linked to the basic principle of all Taoist thought. Merge like with like to create ease, use opposites to generate movement and change, seek to capture a sense of emptiness in order to fill it again with something new, focus on a center point in the midst of activity to maximize the result. No matter the technique used, the end result is an increase in blood circulation, which in turn can relax the muscles and organs and allow a healthy flow of Qi throughout the body.

After rocking for five to ten minutes, or less if the feet have become hot, bring the hands down gracefully in front of the body, palms still facing the

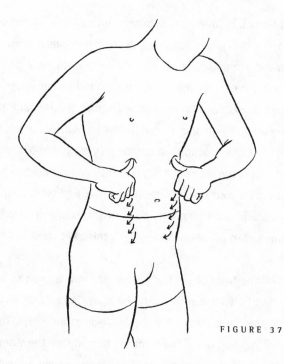

FIGURE 37

chest, until they come to rest in the mudra of peace at the level of the lower *dan tian*. For women, the right hand is placed gently over the left, both palms facing up, with the thumbs natural but slightly elevated, the pads of the thumbs touching lightly. Men place their left hand over their right in the same position. Keep the elbows loose and rounded. Rest in this position for a few moments to allow your Qi and mind to settle and rebalance. If you have experienced any strong memories or emotions while rocking, use this time to mentally savor and digest them. This way you will never forget the insights they have brought.

After composing yourself, move on to the next warm-up exercise. Lean the torso forward slightly to relax the abdominal muscles. In two lines centered with the nipples, beginning right below the rib cage, poke and press into the flesh with the thumbs, alternating them as you work your way down to the crease where the torso meets the top of the leg (Figure 37). Push in relatively firmly, moving the tissue from side to side with each poke. Repeat three times from top to bottom.

Chinese medicine views the spleen and stomach as the body's most basic foundation for day-to-day life. Unlike the kidneys, which are considered your pre-Heavenly foundation, the spleen and stomach are the organs that encapsulate your post-Heavenly foundation. In other words, what your parents gave to you as you were born, all the inherited physical and karmic issues, are expressed through the kidneys. As we've mentioned before, this is your inheritance, your fate, not easily changed or altered in this life without much toil. However, your post-Heaven foundation, what you may make of your life, is developed through the health of the stomach and spleen. Your post-Heaven condition is solely based on your own efforts to improve and build it up. As usual, Taoist practices are focused on providing a means to taking charge of one's life, through one's own efforts, working with the tools most easily at hand.

The two lines down the front of the body massaged in this exercise work on the stomach meridian. Generally, in the body the Yang channels are located along the back, while the Yin channels are mostly located along the front. The only Yang channels running down the front of the body are the stomach meridian's paths. Because of their unique position, they contain an exceptional amount of blood vessels and Qi. Massaging down these paths opens the meridian and breaks up bad Qi and stagnation. As the muscles relax and the circulation improves, eventually you can massage deeper, clearing out debris and blockages in the abdomen and down into the organs. This can relieve constipation and improve the digestion.

Not only does this exercise improve the stomach meridian's condition; it also unifies its function with the other important meridians of the body. This, in turn, can serve to harmonize many aspects of your post-Heaven, everyday life. When poking down the channels with the thumbs, be careful to use the important first point on the lung meridian, which is located directly on the outer side of the thumbnail, right at the edge of the cuticle. As you work your way down, feel the energy of the lung channel flowing through that point and merging with the stomach channel. Remember to keep to the proper breathing pattern. You might feel soreness or tenderness in this area, but breathing regularly and gently will help ease any discomfort.

After using the thumbs down the stomach channel three times from top to bottom, repeat three more times, this time using the heels of the palms.

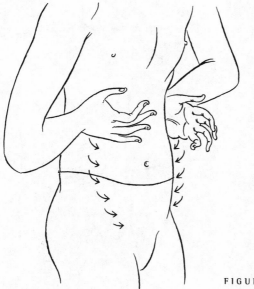

FIGURE 38

Knead down, pushing the flesh from side to side, one palm following the other (Figure 38). Once you reach the mass of flesh under the pubic bone, scoop it up between the palms with a squeeze, then release your hands with a quick outward movement, as if allowing any built-up tension or block in that area to rush out. Men should scoop up the genitalia as part of this squeezing motion, and women should grasp as much of the flesh as they can manage, this area known in Chinese metaphor as the Jade Door. As you press down the channel, use the point right at the center under the first crease of the wrist, where the two mounds of the palm converge. As an important point on the heart meridian, with this next set of three repetitions, you are merging the heart and stomach channels, bringing peace and renewed clarity of purpose to the body and mind. Chinese medicine views an imbalance between the lung and stomach meridians as a common cause of constipation, diarrhea, and other irritable bowel conditions. Heart/stomach meridian imbalance is considered to commonly lead to high blood pressure. With these first two sets of stomach massage, you are helping to settle the interplay of energy between these important networks.

For the final set of three repetitions, the massage technique is slightly

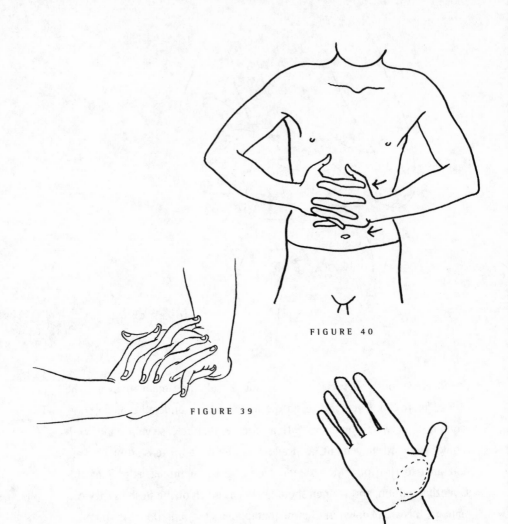

FIGURE 40

FIGURE 39

FIGURE 41

altered. This time, interlace the fingers and "saw" down the abdomen, again working all the way down to the squeeze and release of the pubic mound (Figures 39 and 40). Particularly press in with the center peak of the pad of flesh under the thumb (Figure 41). This point, known as the *yu ji*, or fish belly, stores *jing*. You can tell how much vital essence a person has by the fullness of this part of the palm. The *yu ji* is the point that corresponds to fire on the lung meridian. Harness your fire and natural vitality to energize your stomach massage with this step.

Like the previous two sets, put some pressure onto the direct line of the stomach channels. However, here the clasped hands massage the area between these two lines as well. The motion is back and forth as well as downward. There is a bit of subtlety in this movement, for the back-and-forth pressure isn't on a perfect horizontal line. Instead, trace a flattened figure eight, with its curving, wavelike rhythm, as you work down. As in the torso twists, the figure-eight motion brings dynamic energy to your Qi circulation. With these three sets of stomach channel massage, harmony is brought to a delicate internal system that is easily thrown off balance by daily stress and excitement. It's both stimulating and settling, simple yet highly effective, a perfect example of the power of 9 Palaces Qi Gong.

CULTIVATING THE LOWER DAN TIAN

THERE IS ONE final massage to give yourself, along with the kidney rubbing, the most important in this form. Rubbing the kidneys merges heart and kidney energy, fire and water. It uses opposing energies within the body to create a new force, ready to nourish the growth of the Immortal Fetus. This next massage prepares the lower *dan tian* to become the birthplace of the *Yuan Ying*. Just as a farmer tills the soil before planting a seed, massaging the lower *dan tian* gathers Qi to it, refining it as it is brought in. Yet again, a simple self-massage generates subtle esoteric energies within the body as well as providing beneficial health effects. It's up to you to decide what emphasis you would like to take with your practice, but either way, with daily practice, you are making positive changes in your life.

After the three sets of stomach channel massage, find the lower *dan tian*. As mentioned in Chapter Two, you can determine the area of your lower *dan tian* by forming your hands in a downward-pointing triangle placed over the lower abdomen with the thumbs meeting at the navel. However, as so often is the case in the study of this form, there is a choice of exactly where within this general area you want to concentrate your massage. Commonly, pressure is applied directly to the sensitive point centered between the navel and the top of the pubic bone. With the left hand over the right for women and the right hand over the left for men, use the *yu ji*, or fish belly point on the pad of the palm below the thumb, to press into this point deeply, then massage firmly with a clockwise circular motion. For the first forty-nine days of practice, you can jump-start the cultivation process by massaging below this point, right above the ridge of the pubic bone. There are a number of reasons for this. Sometimes in Chinese medicine, not to mention Taoist healing practices, it is easier to open and unblock an acupuncture point by applying the needle just below or to the side of its actual location. This indirect method more effectively nourishes a point that may be too obstructed or weakened to absorb direct stimulation. Also, by massaging at the top of the pubic bone when first beginning this practice, you will provide a range of benefits not only for the lower *dan tian*, but also for the whole pubic region. These include help for irregular menstruation, menstrual pain, impotence and premature ejaculation. After forty-nine days, moving the massage directly over the center of the lower *dan tian*, will bring maximum Qi into this critical network of blood vessels, nerve endings, and organs, now ready to accept as much energy as you are willing to fill it with.

As we've mentioned before, clockwise movements replenish, while counterclockwise motions disperse. Since the point of this exercise is to bring large amounts of vital Qi to the lower *dan tian*, clockwise massage is always used. Start at the top of the circle, moving to your left and around, always moving as much flesh as you can under your hands, while always focusing the main pressure from the *yu ji* point into the center of the lower *dan tian*. Keep rubbing until the area is painful and hot. Press in as hard as you can without tensing the shoulders or holding the breath. In fact, it's important to remember to breathe in the usual four-and-four rhythm, to ease the exertion of this exercise and help aid the flow of Qi into the lower *dan*. You want it to hurt or feel sore. This will cause heat in the body and a certain amount of endorphin release, which will also increase the amount of Qi rushing straight to that spot. If you can manage it, it's best to do this abdominal massage one hundred times, or even one thousand. Rubbing this vigorously creates a current of electromagnetic energy that is very effective as part of treatment for intestinal and uterine cancers, in fact, for tumors and growths of many kinds throughout the body. Studies coming out of China and Japan, Europe, and now the United States point to a connection between magnetism and the growth and reduction of mutated cells. Enhanced magnetic activity around cancerous cell tissue is in some cases reducing malignancy and even reverting the cellular structure back to normalcy. For Western medicine, these studies are just in their nascence. However, the Taoists have been using basic principles of biomagnetism for thousands of years, to help realign the internal workings of the body.

No matter how many times you rub the lower *dan tian*, this massage cleans the colon and intestines, clears up constipation, aids in weight loss, and brings the digestive system to peak condition. For more serious problems, of course, consult with your doctor, but if you choose to add this massage to your care routine, you must rub for the maximum one thousand revolutions to see the full electromagnetic effect.

The massages over both the pubic bone and the center of the lower *dan tian* tonify a part of the body that normally gets very little attention. The Taoists feel a major reason why women tend to be longer lived than men lies in their ability to bear children. Nine months of pregnancy exercises the pelvic region like nine months of continuously practicing this lower *dan tian* massage. Many women who have serious skin conditions and other chronic and difficult-to-diagnose ailments find that their symptoms clear up during the months of pregnancy, only to return eventually, after the baby is born. On a more esoteric level, when a woman becomes pregnant, she increases her longevity by carrying heavenly Qi inside her womb as the fetus develops. This is no less cultivation of the lower *dan tian* than a life of Qi Gong practice. A Taoist nun Dr. Wu had known from childhood surprised him a number of years ago by admitting to him that when she was younger, she intentionally broke the vows of her order to have a child. She wanted her chance to cultivate heavenly Qi, no matter what sacrifices she had to make. After the child was born, she gave it up for adoption, returned to her nunnery, and hadn't breathed a word of what she had done for many years. Today she is still performing her vows at the ripe age of 109. Men and childless women needn't worry that they are missing out on an opportunity for energetic cultivation.

Daily practice of this circular lower *dan tian* massage will bring a new quality of energy into this important seat of health and longevity. It's up to you to create the foundation for your *Yuan Ying* to spring to life.

THE NINE CLEANSING BREATHS

AT THIS POINT, the body has been completely warmed through and the Qi and blood circulation are activated. Now it's time to start exchanging Qi with the universe, while absorbing and balancing all the internal energy created by this long set of warm-ups. Many Taoist alchemical texts make reference to "Qi Bathing." Yet again, far from being some sort of arcane mental meditation or philosophy, a basic breathing exercise is all that's needed to accomplish this supposed mystery (Figure 42).

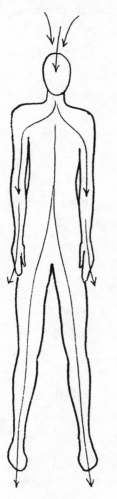

Stand with your arms gently hanging at your sides. Check your feet to make sure they are still pointing straight ahead or slightly inward, legs shoulder-width apart. Begin lightly inhaling through the nose, gradually filling the entire rib cage with air. At the same time as you are bringing air up through your nose and elevating your rib cage as it expands with your breath, imagine pulling heavenly Qi down into the top of the head through the *ba hui* point, roughly analogous to the crown chakra. You can find the exact spot of your *ba hui* point by tracing imaginary lines from the highest points on the tops of the ears and another line from the tip of the nose until all three meet together at the center top of the head. This is one of the most important points in the body, physically and esoterically, often referred to as the point where "one hundred channels meet together." There is a great

FIGURE 42

concentration of Yang channels in the top of the head. Refining them allows us to sense our environment more fully and exchange communication with the universe. The *ba hui* point, as the "Yang within the Yang," is the vital point from where the *Yuan Ying* can flow freely up to unite with its other half in the heavens. Conversely, in Chinese medical treatment, this is a prime point of moxibustion for symptoms of chronic fatigue. We bring in healing Qi through this point to revitalize and detoxify the entire body.

Inhale slowly and fully through the nose while bringing Heavenly Qi down through the *ba hui* point. Do not inhale to the point where you begin to hold your breath. This is a powerful breathing exercise, and you must go gently to avoid an unpleasant "head rush." When you have come close to the limit of your inhale and your rib cage is rounded front and back with air, swallow all this Qi and air down to the lower *dan tian*. Use an actual physical swallowing movement. You will find that this incorporates important muscles down through the torso, past the diaphragm, into the abdomen, not unlike how a snake swallows its prey. Over time, as your body gets accustomed to this action, you may make the swallowing less physically pronounced. Do what comes most naturally to maximize your practice. As you swallow the Qi to the lower *dan tian*, exhale through the mouth very slowly, totally relaxed. Feel the Qi still pouring down through your *ba hui* point, across the shoulders, down the arms, and out each finger. Also feel the Qi continuing downward from the lower *dan tian*, splitting across the pelvis, down the legs, and out the toes and the centers of the soles of the feet, and also out the urethra and anus. Remember, the urethra connects with the

FIGURE 43

stomach, bladder, and uterus. The anus connects with the intestines. Every part of your body is being opened and cleansed. Feel as if you are bathing in a shower of Qi, all the stagnant energy passing out of the body, replaced by new, vital Qi (Figure 43). The exhale is the most important part of this exercise. The Qi doesn't stop anywhere in the body. It just comes as a flow of warmth, then passes out. At the point where you have no more breath to exhale, repeat again from the inhale, for nine total repetitions. Don't go too slowly. This exercise should be invigorating and refreshing as well as relaxing. You are replacing your Qi.

Qi Bathing training is an exceptional detoxifier and rebalancer for the entire body. Dr. Wu teaches it to his AIDS and cancer patients to practice alongside their Western and Eastern medical treatment, to very noticeable effect. The toes are related to the head, their opposite. They are the poles of the body, north and south, Yin and Yang. This exercise keeps the magnetic pull between them in balance. Also, illness leaves the body from three places: one-third from the hands, one-third from the feet, and the final third from the bodily wastes. You help stimulate this natural elimination process, reoxegenating the body and internally massaging the organs with your breath and the fresh Qi you take in from above. Qi flows all around us, but Qi Gong practice creates a rhythm between our bodies and this perpetual flow. Further, the inside of our bodies makes important decisions for us. By cleansing the 9 Palaces, we combine the Human with the Heavens. Open your meridians and be free from all pain.

THE SECOND HEART

THE CELEBRATED HUA Tuo, eminent doctor and scholar of the Han Dynasty, developed the famous Five Animal Exercises as a surefire method of maintaining inner and outer health. Part one of 9 Palaces Qi Gong concludes with one of the two-thousand-year-old exercises from this set. Place the hands back in position over the lower *dan tian*, the same as when beginning the lower *dan* massage. Women place the left hand over the right, men the right over the left, covering the abdomen over the lower *dan tian*. Standing straight and tall, kick down the center of the back of the left calf with the edge of the right foot (Figure 44). Kick firmly, using plenty of force, working from the back of the knee straight down to the ankle. Repeat nine times from top to bottom, then switch sides for nine more repeats, the edge of the left foot kicking the right calf. This is known as the Golden Rooster Standing on One Leg. Heavy toxins in the body tend to settle in this critical area from calf to ankle. The stomach channel and the spleen channel are found on either side of the calf muscle. Due to gravity's perpetual influence, the heaviest residues accumulate here, clogging the circulation. The Taoists see this area as so critical to the body's health that, it is referred to as the Second Heart. In Taoist medicine, if there are problems with the heart, this is the area that is treated. If you consistently practice the Golden Rooster exercise, it can help you gain health for your heart. This kicking is a wonderful self-massage, and the process of standing on one leg augments its effects by training your sense of

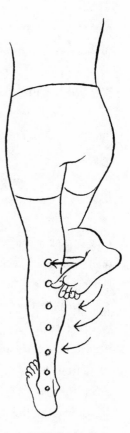

FIGURE 44

your body's alignment and center of gravity. Standing tall and looking straight ahead, feeling the body pulled up and the torso perfectly placed over the hips, will help you keep your balance while finely adjusting your posture. In fact, this basic exercise is one of the classic foundation trainings for Tai Chi mastery. The straighter you stand, the more easily the sediment in the body will find its way down, ready to be massaged out. If it's difficult to maintain a standing posture while kicking the calves, by all means use one hand to lean against a wall or tree while you keep the other over the lower *dan tian*. With daily practice, you will strengthen yourself, though, so it really is worthwhile to try bit by bit to get through the nine repetitions on each side standing on one leg. As usual, keeping the proper four-and-four breathing will make the exercise go a lot easier.

We know that birds can fly high but on land who can run faster than the horse? Sometimes horses can run for a hundred miles before exhausting themselves. If you watch them carefully, you will see that they kick the backs of their legs in a very similar way to this exercise to relieve their fatigue. What we are attempting is to imitate the animals' natural behavior to recover from our own tiredness. If you are buying a horse and spot one that is kicking its shins, you're going to know that that horse will be an excellent runner. It's showing its natural instinct to balance and regulate itself. Right now, by doing the Golden Rooster exercise, we are balancing ourselves, relaxing from all the day's excitement, calming ourselves down.

If at any time you feel fatigue, such as after a long hike or being on your feet all day, if you feel a tightness or sensation of expansion over the heart, or if your body feels a bit swollen and tender, you can practice the calf-kicking to relieve the tiredness and discomfort.

After the Golden Rooster practice, we have completed the first section of 9 Palaces Qi Gong. We have awakened the circulation of blood and Qi from head to toe and loosened all the joints, where Qi accumulates and in turn flows from. You should feel warm, light, and streaming with energy. This may seem like a lot of work, but it needn't be time-consuming. As you become accustomed to the form, this whole series of warm-ups shouldn't take more than twenty minutes from the ears to the feet and calves. Keeping a good pace while practicing will energize the body, give you a good cardiovascular workout, and still leave you in a state of calm relaxation. If you are extremely pressed for time, just do the hand-shaking, kidney-rubbing, and lower *dan tian* massage before proceeding to the next section. Know that you can do any of these exercises separately at any time of the day, whenever you need a little lift. Whether you are taking a quick break behind your desk at the office or standing on a cliff overlooking the ocean, make 9 Palaces Qi Gong yours. Healing begins in the mind and the heart and leads to becoming one with Heaven and Earth.

SIX

Opening the Heavenly Eye

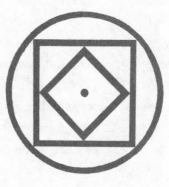

THE THIRD EYE—these three words represent rare and powerful knowledge, sought throughout the history of humanity. As far back as mankind's prehistoric past, the science of human consciousness has been rigorously studied the world over, always linked with opening the mind to new states of awareness. Every race, every culture, in every generation, has toiled to attain the precious sacrament of psychic and spiritual attainment.

Unfortunately, equally far back, its study has been suppressed or coopted by those greedy for control over the common man. Many who attempted to preserve the teachings were oppressed, driven underground, or persecuted to the point of death. Charlatans sprang up, seeking personal gain as they hoodwinked eager students anxious to believe. Myths and fears were fabricated to further dissuade those who would wish to learn, both by the powers that be and by the keepers of the teachings themselves. As secrecy and misinformation took hold, true methods of psychic development gradually died out, fading into obscurity and then oblivion. How much blood was shed in Europe, the Middle East, Africa, Asia, and the Americas to wipe out all traces of the truth? Today, once-powerful mystical traditions limp along, their lineages broken or scattered, their teachings altered beyond recognition. Such has been the history of the human grasp for a higher plane of existence.

Still, people continue the search. The lure of magical vistas, not visible to the physical eye, is too strong to let go. The Third Eye, able to see all that is hidden, is to this day a source of endless fascination, intellectual debate, and eager searching. What is the pull of opening the Heavenly Eye, this hold its secret has on our imagination, which has caused so many to risk so much? Despite all the advances of the modern world, why do people still seek the miraculous?

Could it be that these mysteries have held mankind's attention for thousands of years because they contain an element of truth? Do we yearn for psychic awareness not as a means of creating the impossible, but out of a subconscious drive to express the full capacity of the human mind? The Taoists have always recognized that the development of the mind's untapped potential is equal in importance to promoting physical health. Techniques were formulated over generations of study to unlock abilities within the brain that were seen as a natural step in the journey of becoming a fully realized person. The ancient masters and their wisdom went through the same process of persecution and dilution, and yet, within the confines of the monasteries, the traditions were held safe for many generations.

However, even with centuries of tightly held tradition, the practice of the 9 Palaces had nearly been forgotten in the White Cloud Monastery. While the Yin Qi Gong form known as the 5 Centers had been maintained in its entirety since the founding of the monastery, by the early twentieth century there was a consensus within the ranks of the orders represented there that something would need to be done to revive the 9 Palaces. For this purpose, Dr. Wu's master was appointed by his order in the south of China to travel north to Beijing, as the emissary of its last remaining unbroken lineage. The 9 Palaces training set forth here is a rare prize, a system of development of mind and consciousness as well as body and health, untouched over a thousand years of history, a time capsule of the world of the ancient men of wisdom.

Of course, not everyone interested in the study of Qi Gong pursues it for esoteric reasons. The health benefits of daily practice are more than enough to convince many to make it a part of their daily routine. This is not to say that a quickening of awareness, a sensation of contemplative peace, may not come over the regular practitioner, no matter what his or her original interest may have been. Taoist thought does not make a separation between the cosmic order and the internal order of the body. As above, so below, a basic tenet of mystical teachings the world over, applies intimately to 9 Palaces Qi Gong. In the second section of the 9 Palaces form, we will focus on unblocking and opening the pathways of energy between the internal organs, the five senses, the outer world, and beyond to the inner reaches of perception.

Now that the circulation has been enhanced and the muscles and joints warmed and loosened, standing postures aided by visualization take the loosening and warming process deeper into the structure of the body. For those inclined to see visualization as an unnecessary gloss over a basically physical function, be aware that the visualizations involved in 9 Palaces Qi Gong work as subtle enhancements to the effort of the standing postures they accompany. Simply put, think of this section as a series of isometric exercises in reverse, working from the inner surfaces of bone and connective tissue outward toward the muscle. While you visualize sending your senses far out past the normal limit of perception, you will find that tiny muscles around the spot being concentrated on will strain, twitch, or get warm with exertion. Rest assured that you are exercising key muscles around the eyes, ears, nose, and mouth, as well as stimulating the portions of the brain that govern their function with this specifically chosen imagery. It is perfectly valid to eventually eliminate the visual component of these postures as the body gets used to how they feel. In fact, experiencing Qi Gong on the purely somatic level will lead to even greater control and beneficial results. Just as a dancer's or singer's training leads to grace of movement or richness of voice in day-to-day life, Qi Gong practice tones little-used muscles and neural pathways for detoxifying and regulating one's health. But a dancer doesn't dance just to stay in shape, and most people who practice 9 Palaces Qi Gong discover that this holds true for themselves as well. This is clearing the mind to encounter the soul, brought down to the level of physical sensation and personal expression.

"As large as infinity, as small as a grain of sand" is a key concept in Taoist thought. This is not just a statement of humility in the face of an infinite universe. The Taoist practitioner strives to achieve flexible states of perception that can expand outward to gather energy and information from all around, or shrink inward to make changes on the deepest cellular level. With each posture in the second part of the 9 Palaces form, we are going to explore capabilities of the five senses that at first glance seem beyond the range of normal experience. Over time, the Heavenly Eye that reads the messages of the universe can open in any of us. The beauty of 9 Palaces Qi Gong is that at every step of the way, you are helping yourself on a physical and emotional level. The esoteric awareness and mystical insights follow naturally of their own accord, often emerging in a surprising way, when least expected. This practice is also known as the Healthy and Happy Gong, for it is a Qi Gong form specifically focused on healing and detoxifying the body. However, there's no way of dancing around the fact that many people who start practicing this form on a regular basis bring extraordinary experiences into their lives. Is it because new neural pathways are being created in the brain due to these very specific exercises? Would you prefer to attach a spiritual or religious significance to the changes that take place in one's consciousness? How do you choose to perceive them? By accepting what comes to you during these postures, not trying to endlessly repeat moments that may only come once, always learning from them and knowing there is always yet more to learn. This is the path to harmony with the universe.

SENDING THE EYES OUT

EVERYONE KNOWS THE old homily that "the eyes are the windows of the soul." The Taoists also have always recognized this important truism. It doesn't matter what clothes you wear or what image you try to display, the eyes reveal one's true self to those who can see. The moon in the sky, along with the eyes, bright as the moon, are reflections of the heart. After the sense of touch, eyesight is the very first way we interact with the world around us, from earliest infancy. We spend a lot of time sending our sight out to look at all the stimulating things that surround us in our daily lives. The Taoists believe that sometimes we might even see things that were not meant for our eyes and bring in sickness and bad luck because of it. Whether you believe this or not, there is a point to be made when we consider how little we consciously internalize the information we are continually bombarding our eyes with. There's no doubt that the sense of sight takes in input that can affect us subconsciously, just as surely as staring at a computer screen all day can make the whole body feel tired. A monk living within the confines of a quiet monastery might simply choose to look at fewer things to keep in good order. Getting through the week in the hectic modern world certainly makes this a luxury few of us can afford. Taking time to clean and refresh our visual pipeline, besides preventing stresses that could negatively impact our health if not monitored, gives us more space to engage in a deeper communication with the world around us.

For thousands of years, Chinese medicine has recognized the connection between the liver and the eyes, considering that one reflects the condition of the other. Even Western medicine acknowledges this relationship to a certain extent. The first indicator of hepatitis is a yellow cast to the whites of the eyes. The skin becomes sallow only as the disease progresses. This exercise clears the eye/liver channel of obstructions, promoting healing in a whole range of eye and liver conditions, such as hepatitis, chronic fatigue (related to the liver), eyestrain, cataracts, and glaucoma. The liver is the most important organ in a woman's body. Its health will be an indicator of her entire body's health. No matter with what problems a female patient comes to Dr. Wu for treatment, he will always include some care for her liver. According to Taoist healing food theories, adding a little liver to one's diet is beneficial for a weak liver and certain eye conditions, goat liver being the best, followed by cow, pig, chicken, and duck liver, in order of effectiveness. The Five Elements nourish and control one another. The liver is green, the heart is red, the spleen yellow, the lungs white, and the kidneys black. In general, eating foods the color of the organ you wish to treat is a basic Taoist health practice, relating back to finding harmony by pairing like Qi with like. Looking at these colors with the eyes will also enhance treatment. White radish soup is good for the lungs. Eggplant is given for impotence, related to the kidneys. Red relieves the blood. A heart patient might consider laying down carpet with a little red mixed into it, so it can catch the eye throughout the day. Green will have a positive effect on the heart as well as red, because its corresponding wood element relating to the liver supports the heart's fire element in the generative cycle of the Five Elements. For men, longevity is related to the kidneys. For women, the liver should always be the first priority when seeking a long life. Eating green food and looking at green things is particularly helpful for women trying to maintain their livers.

In Five Elements theory, the element of wood is associated with the liver. The eye/liver meridian exercise is considered a Wood Practice. As wood controls Earth and the eyes are the middlemen between the liver and the universe, starting the second section of the 9 Palaces Qi Gong with this practice firmly establishes a person's place standing between Heaven and Earth. From the basic standing posture, slowly raise the hands up, arms gently bent, palms facing toward the body, to just above eye level, with the pinkies aligned with the eyebrows. Keep the eyes closed and the breathing steady. From behind your closed eyelids, imagine your eyes opening and looking outward to the centers of the palms. Feel the eyes looking straight through the palms and out into the room (Figure 45). Try to see the room around you. Continue looking up to the ceiling, then farther up, right through the ceiling and the roof, then up and out, high above the city streets. Keep sending your eyes outward all the way to the edge of the ocean, then farther still to the distant horizon. You might feel a sensation that your eyes want to pull back into your head.

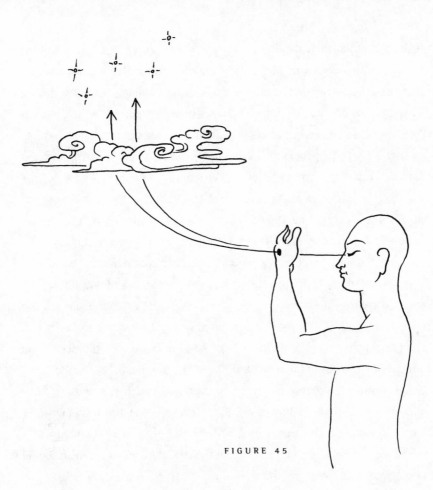

FIGURE 45

Just breathe into it gently and give them an extra push farther out instead. Continue looking up, through the blue sky and the white clouds, all the way into outer space.

At this point you need to start looking farther, but now not only with the two eyes on your face, but also with your third eye, known by the Taoists as the Heavenly Eye or *tian ying*. Unfurl your Heavenly Eye, as a rose would open its petals, right between the eyes at brow level. Try and see what you can with it. Join your third eye with your two physical eyes to continue looking out through space. If you can't see anything with the third eye, no matter. Just keep looking out, breathing with the four-and-four rhythm, past the moon, then past the sun, then past the edge of the solar system. Just as before, if you feel any of your eyes wanting to pull back in, don't let them.

Push them out again just a little farther. By now, it's very common to feel the muscles and tendons around the eyes straining and twitching, not unlike a bicep would toward the end of a set of weight training. Just keep looking outward, all the way to the edge of the universe. Then push past the edge of the universe and behold what lies beyond it. There are certain things that frequently are seen by people at this point, but rather than list them, suffice it to say that each person's experience is different.

Once you have extended your sight through your palms and past the edge of the universe (this should take about two to three minutes), start to more quickly pull your three eyes back. Bring them back past to this solar system, past the sun, then past the moon. Just as you continuously pushed your vision outward, try to bring your sight back in one steady draw, not letting the solid column of energy diffuse. Once you get back to outer space, close your Heavenly Eye and continue downward with your two physical eyes. Pull them again past the white clouds and the blue sky, across the ocean and through the city. Bring them down through the roof and back into the room. Gradually draw the eyes to the center of the palms, which by now should feel hot. Gently bring the palms to cover the eyes, feeling the heat permeate them as you place them back in their sockets. This heat is a healing force from the universe, Heavenly Qi. Bringing the eyeballs back to the head should take about thirty seconds. There is no need to go too slowly or get lost within this practice. Keep a focused pace. Leave the palms covering the eyes until the eyeballs feel cool and very comfortable. As you feel the energy flow from your palms to your eyes, visualize the color green. Not only are you healing and refreshing your eyes, the process of sending your gaze out to the edge of the universe and back again is a special cultivation for your eyes to gain the wisdom of seeing relationships in their right light.

Now it's time to replenish the liver with this same Heavenly Qi. Feel the warmth from the palms pass through the eyes and down into your liver. (Figure 46). Keep thinking of the color green as you send a steady stream of energy into your liver. As the energy flows in, picture your liver shrinking and shrinking until it is so small it disappears. Savor the concept of "larger than infinity, smaller than a grain of sand" you have just enacted. Then remove your palms from your eyes and place them directly over your liver until you feel comfortable. If you taste a sour flavor like a salted plum in your mouth at this point, you will know you have succeeded in completely opening your liver meridian. If you don't taste it at first, you can start the whole exercise from the beginning again, or just keep practicing daily. With the completion of this posture, you will have experienced what the Taoists refer to as Heaven and Human United as One. With the Heavenly Qi flowing through your liver, you have increased your organ's poten-

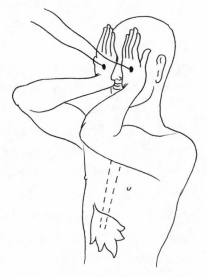

FIGURE 46

tial for communication with the outside world. In the Tao, it is believed that everyone is also a star up in the sky. Every organ in your body finds its ultimate expression in communication with this star that is you.

THE HEAVENLY EYE

THE EYES IN our head can see whatever appears in front of them. The Heavenly Eye has the ability to see things that are beyond the reach of the physical eyes, things that coexist with us on different planes of awareness. It can also perceive things that do exist here but are impossible for the naked eye to see, such as disease within the body, or people or places that are far away. Does the third eye really exist? Historically, the third eye has been linked to the pineal gland. Located near the center of the brain, this small endocrine gland secretes melatonin, regulating seasonal charges in the metabolism and reproductive function, as well as affecting the circadian rhythms of the body. Extended studies of the pineal gland in Japan, which have been met with a positive level of acceptance by the scientific community, show both in its components and functions, the pineal gland is remarkably similar to the eye, as its neurochemical compositon has certain light-detecting properties that control the production of melatonin. There is some disagreement as to whether the pineal gland shares the same full abilities of our eyesight. However, with his background in research neurophysiology, Dr. Wu feels these studies are conclusive enough to be accepted.

Dr. Wu has other reasons to give credence to the existence of the Heavenly Eye. When visiting monasteries in Tibet as a young man with his teacher, Dr. Wu had the opportunity to witness the surgical procedure the lamas use to open the third eye. Using special medicinal leaves, the skin over the third eye was rubbed continuously for one to two days, until the skin was broken and the soft bone behind it had completely dissolved. Then herbal poultices were applied to make sure the skin would heal back over the hole. If the lama was very lucky, the skin would grow back and he would be capable of remarkable feats of X-ray vision. Dr. Wu tried to test an older lama by offering him a cigarette from his pack if he could tell him how many cigarettes were left inside. Not only did the old monk tell him how many cigarettes were left; he gave him a listing down to the last coin of all the other things in his pockets. Unfortunately, the lamas always ran the risk of the wound not healing, which could easily lead to death. Whether with the leaf technique or with actual trepanation (surgically drilling openings in the skull), the risks involved so heavily outweigh the benefits, it only serves to illustrate the pull of the knowledge possibly to be gained: so strong as to make its seekers dare to lose their lives.

The Taoists have other techniques for opening the Heavenly Eye, none of which have ever before been revealed to the public. Obviously, they are much safer, being nonsurgical. They are simple, yet highly effective, for they harmonize the body's natural abilities with the seasons and rhythms of the world. The very first thing to be aware of, if your intention is to unlock this ability, is the time of the year to practice to achieve results. Sometimes people come to Dr. Wu wondering why they have yet to experience the opening of the Heavenly Eye, even though they have meditated for eight or ten years. It was simply because they didn't start their practice in its right season. You must start in the fall, about one lunar month before the Chinese Lunar Festival, somewhere between August and September, depending on the year. Just as we harvest our crops in the autumn, when they have reached their peak of ripe perfection, you must harvest the innate capabilities of the third eye at this same time. No other time of the year will do. Earlier, and your body will not be ready; later, and winter's "killing force" will be upon you, drawing your energy down too deep within. Also, for the same reasons, practice only between four in the afternoon and nine in the evening, the most autumnal hours of the day. While starting or continuing your practice at the wrong time of the year or day is not damaging to the body, the practitioner may not achieve successful results.

While the eye/liver meridian practice of the 9 Palaces will greatly enhance your physical eyesight and stabilize the energy of your Heavenly Eye, to reach a more advanced level that strictly focuses on opening the Third Eye, follow these steps as a separate exercise from your 9 Palaces Qi Gong practice. Lay a white cloth over a square-topped stool or low card table. You want the stool or table to be low enough that when you stand before it, you can look down easily and see its whole surface without having to bend the head down or position the eyes in any other way than a natural, relaxed downward gaze.

In Taoist cosmology, the regions of the head and face have been assigned a correspondence with the outer world. From the eyebrows to the indentation above the lip is Human. From the indentation over the lip to the chin is the Ocean. From the browline up is your Heaven. First gaze upon the white square with your eyes for a moment, trying to absorb what you are seeing into your Heaven as well as your eyes. Then close your eyes and try to see the white square of the tabletop with only your Heaven. Even though you are using the top of the head from the browline up to sense this image, you will be triggering your Heavenly Eye, opening it up for it to do the looking. If you have the base ability to open your third eye, after a few moments of this, a square image that moves with the light and rhythm of the snowy static on a blank television screen will come into view on your brow. If you can see this sparkling square after nine full repetitions of extending the eyes out, bringing them back in, and staring at the white square with eyes open and shut, you know you have the aptitude to go forward with opening your Heavenly Eye. Don't think this is a rare talent. Certainly, there's an element of aptitude here, just as some people are naturally better athletes or musicians. Some people can fully open their third eye in a few days or even hours of this practice. On average you should be able to manage it with one hundred days of practice, based on normal brain function.

Once you are able to easily get the "screen" across your Heaven into focus, you can start giving yourself further challenges. Instead of an empty white cloth, lay a small, simple object (a pencil is ideal) in its center. Continue practicing in the same way, trying to fix the image of the pencil first with the eyes, then within the screen of the Heavenly Eye. This may not sound very easy, but you would be surprised at how the proper timing, combined with these trainings, will help get you on your way. Once seeing the pencil within the Third Eye becomes effortless, try breaking the pencil within your mind. See it snapping apart, as if you were looking at it with your physical eyes. This is quite powerful. You will certainly know when you have accomplished it.

After this stage, try doing this practice outside without a white square. Instead, train your Heavenly Eye on an ant crawling along the ground. See if you can get it to stop in its tracks with the force from your Heavenly Eye's gaze. One of Dr. Wu's students puts it this way: "I finished my 9 Palaces practice in the park one day and felt it was suddenly the right moment to try this out. As I looked down on the ground, my attention landed on one particular ant that was part of a column marching along. I felt very connected with this ant. The connection definitely came from my Heavenly Eye more than from anywhere else. The ant's feelers went up and it stopped dead in its tracks, like it was held there by a force field. I stared fascinated at this for a few moments, but then I felt a pang of conscience, because I could sense the ant calling out in confusion to its mates still crawling along in the row, while it was stuck and couldn't move. I had the feeling I could have held it in its spot for as long as I wanted, but I broke the connection with my mind because I felt it wasn't my right to hold a little ant from going about its business." Once you get to this level of ability, you know you have trained quite well.

What will you bring into your life by opening the Heavenly Eye? Each person is different. Some people experience uncanny events and insights that are hard to find a rational explanation for. Others find a deepened connection to nature and their friends and family. Suffice it to say, opportunities to help others with your newly enhanced perception will come your way, without having to run looking for them. Certainly, opening the Heavenly Eye is a very specialized technique. Whether or not you choose to delve this deeply, know that Qi Gong, practiced with sincerity, benefits not only yourself, but reaches out in positive ways to all you come in contact with. Harmonizing Human with Heaven, we cannot help but share something positive with everything around us.

RU YI

AFTER THE EYES and liver are opened and nourished, the next posture turns to the stomach and spleen. As said before, the spleen and stomach are key organs that reflect and influence our daily lives in the most basic ways. According to Chinese medicine, the spleen and stomach are both digestive organs and store water. Muscle growth is governed by the stomach and spleen. By extension, muscle pain is also related to the stomach and spleen. The spleen's Qi rises upward. The stomach's Qi falls downward. Together, they hold the central element of Earth within the body. They are the mothers of the body, balancing every part of its structure and all the rest of the organs with their flow of Yin and Yang. When healing the body, proper food is better than medicine and Qi is better than food. This is the essence of nutrition. Practice this with mind and body. The stomach is emotional. The task is to keep it relaxed and resting quietly. The next exercise helps preserve the delicate balance of stomach and spleen from the stresses and strains of everyday life.

After finishing the eye/liver opening, bring the hands, palms up, to rest in the crease formed where the torso meets the tops of the thighs. Placing the palms upward, you are preserving Qi. As usual, keep the elbows softly rounded. Begin swaying gently in a figure-eight motion, starting from left to right. Lead with your shoulders, feeling your entire torso integrated into this soft movement. Feel as if you are a lotus, swaying in the breeze. Your body from the waist down has become your roots reaching deep into the mud at the bottom of the lake. Your torso is the lotus's strong and flexible stem. Your arms are the rounded leaves, skimming the surface of the water. Your head is the lotus flower, and in the center, the seed pod is your brain. Allow your whole body to join in the rhythm of the figure-eight swaying, shifting your weight from leg to leg as you lead into the wavelike motion.

The movement of this exercise is like mixing medicine in a bottle. You are swirling your own internal medicines within the vessel of your lower *dan tian*. Mix it well to allow the body to regulate. There is a popular type of dim sum that is rolled into a flaky, multilayered ball by shaking the dough in a cupped hand. As it rolls and bounces around, it grows layer by layer until it is ready to be cooked. This is the same way the Chinese mix herbs into medicine. Western medicine tends to pound and process. The Chinese use the shaking method in order to produce a ball. In basketball, the players pass the ball around before they shoot, in order to build a rhythm and feeling in the ball. This helps them calm, control, and focus before they make the shot. This same theory is used in making traditional Chinese medicine. Dr. Wu has viewed high-tech Western-style pharmaceutical factories in Japan. The processing is very mechanical. The shaking method is more natural, using raw, unprocessed herbs in small, safe doses.

Keep this in mind as you sway from side to side. Become aware of the spleen and stomach energy rising and falling within the body. Breathe in as you move from left to right feeling the sensation of your spleen Qi sinking downward. Breathe out as you feel your stomach Qi pushed upward, moving from right to left. You are working your stomach and spleen energies up and down, exercising the Qi vertically and horizontally at the same time. This makes them stronger and more easily able to self-regulate. This practice is the twin to Crossing the Bridge in the first section of the form, described in chapter Five. All the movements are done gently. If you have to focus less on the breathing and just get deeper into the rhythm of the sway, by all means do so. You will find that all these motions will integrate themselves perfectly over time. Just experience the sensation of gently rising and falling energies as your weight shifts while you sway.

What ties them all together? There is a very particular state of mind that you must allow to take over when practicing the stomach swaying. In Chinese, it's known as *yangyang zhide*: "I am number one!" Think of things that make you so happy you want to smile from ear to ear. Feel proud of yourself, successful, maybe even a touch arrogant, like a noble lord or lady surveying the kingdom. Once a year in the White Cloud Monastery, all the monks would assemble together in the main courtyard, arrayed in their finest robes, to practice this swaying exercise together. Don't underestimate this simple detail. Just as stress can negatively impact the stomach and slowly create a negative environment for disease to appear, positive thoughts, combined with relaxing movement, foster a change for the better in health as well as behavior. Just as illness forms slowly and subtly out of intangible stresses, good luck and desired outcomes can spring from a successful state of mind. This swaying combined with the feeling of being on top of the world can help you to achieve whatever your heart desires.

A young patient came to Dr. Wu. He felt that at thirty-two, he had so far been very unlucky in meeting women. He joked with Dr. Wu, saying, "Since I'm practicing the 9 Palaces, do you have any special movements I can add to find myself a steady girlfriend?" Dr. Wu told him that this exercise was all he needed. He just had to sway, feeling great about himself. His motion would catch the right girl for him within its flow. The figure-eight swaying motion is called the Eight Fairy Gods Within the Turning Point. The number 8 indicates success and all going smoothly. A traditional ornamental talisman of good luck is called Ru Yi, for bringing in the heart's wishes, and this practice is known in Chinese as Ru Yi Gong. This may seem simplistic, but there's no doubt that your ability to be successful is based on your daily behavior.

It's easy to do one good thing in one's life. Doing good consistently until the end of your days is not quite so simple. Or course, we can all say we accomplished a few kind acts. They're easy to remember and easy to list. But if we do wrong, do we willingly remember our actions quite so easily? What's the dividing line between your good deeds and your bad deeds? Doing good, you are helping other people, making them happy. Harming other people to benefit yourself is wrong. The Taoists recognize the importance of feeling good about oneself, but provide a context of healing and well-wishing to instill a positive outcome.

Ru Yi Gong is simple. Think of the things you're most proud of or accomplishments you want to be successful in attaining. Keep swaying, training the stomach and spleen. You have to make the figure eight as you sway, rotating around your central core, building up force inside your body, taking in and sending out energy in one fluid motion. In your mind you're thinking of the next couple of days, the things you need to do, the outcomes that you have to achieve. Studies have shown that if you look at a house plant every day and tell it with your mind to grow and be healthy, it will bloom vigorously. If, on the other hand, you tell it daily to die, it will weaken and shrivel, even if you give it the same amount of water and sunlight as the first plant. Everything around us retains memories of the impact its environment has upon it. With Ru Yi Gong, you are sending out a mental impulse, a brain wave, if you will. Send out this thought form to a friend you wish well, or toward a project you would like to see succeed.

Gradually your results will go in the direction you willed them. Don't underestimate this concept. Remember that not only are you thinking positive thoughts during this practice, you are moving in harmony with the universe, setting up a wave of energy with the rotation of your body. On a purely physiological level, you will find that maintaining a feeling of pride and grandeur while swaying will actually help you keep the energy you are generating in your body, by focusing your movements upward toward your head as you sway. This has a stimulating and refreshing effect that merely swaying without directing the energy would not have. It's a very good example of how visualization and directed emotion indeed affect the perception of energy within the body. Test it for yourself.

There is one last aspect of the Ru Yi Gong that returns to opening the Heavenly Eye. While this practice is done for longevity and health, there is something more you can add if you wish to go further and prepare a foundation for the achievement of the Rainbow Body, as did Dr. Wu's saintly teacher. After swaying long enough to feel completely enmeshed in the rhythm of the movement, feel as if you are standing in the center of a pyramid. Begin to visualize a circle with no beginning or end on the expanse of your heavenly screen above brow level. After a moment, picture a square inside the circle, a diamond shape within the square and then at last, a point at the cen-

FIGURE 47

ter of the diamond (Figure 47). Keep swaying and hold steady to this point for a few extra seconds. Then start over visualizing the circle, the square within the circle, the diamond and the point again. Continue forming and reforming this diagram, each time holding steady on the final point in the center for a few moments, swaying your body in its figure eight the whole time. There is no set amount of times to do this. Just continue until when you hold your attention on the central point, you feel your body is rising up, your feet trying to lift themselves off the ground, as if an electrical shock is surging through your body, making you want to jump up. If you get this sensation, you know you have practiced with the proper concentration.

This symbol is used by advanced martial artists to strike a crushing blow to their opponents. As you approach to attack, you imagine your sparring partner surrounded by the circle, the circle and the person merging together as a whole. Then, within this space, see the square on the torso, the diamond around the area of the heart point, or middle *dan*, and the point right in the very center of the chest. In Taoist terms, you have "covered" your opponent. As you practice T'ai Chi Push Hands with your partner, power will build up around this central point and you will push in with great electrical force and win your match without having to expend much physical effort. Though much has been spoken of Wang Xiangzhai's famous Lightning Force Kung Fu, you won't read this detail in any book. And yet this was the core of his martial arts mastery. Ten men could jump on him all at once and he could repel them all in a flash. He would keep this force coiled within him, ready to strike out in a burst of electrical energy. If his opponents tried to touch him, they would get a shock, as if from a stun gun. This is not an aberration. His abilities were achieved through long years of practice unlocking something that was already there. There is the thought that the moment you are born, the force with which you rush from the womb is the same as this strong bioelectric force generated with the symbol and swaying of Ru Yi Gong. In other words, everyone has this power inside him- or herself. Once you think about these four elements, the circle, square, diamond, and point, the force inside you should automatically come out. The strength within yourself and the strength of the universe combine, like a key opening a lock that releases a great primal power.

The other crucial element to remember when perfecting the practice of Ru Yi Gong is imagining yourself at the center of a pyramid. What exactly is this pyramid? Certainly there have been many interesting studies of the preservative properties of the pyramid. From ancient Egyptian mummies to fresh food and flowers, there seems to be a remarkable slowing of the deterioration process in organic objects placed directly at the center of a pyramid. The Chinese have a parallel way of looking at this. First of all, many of the body's components form pyramids. The shoulders and head, the shoulders down to the groin, the hips up to the top of the head, as well as the testes and penis, all echo the pyramid. The pyramid represents pure Yang force. But to achieve this energy, you must envision the circle first. The day before Master Du attained the Rainbow Body, he spoke at length on the topic of embodying a circle of energy that becomes a pyramid. This is the pyramid you want to stand beneath while you practice Ru Yi Gong. If you can accomplish this, you will begin the formation of your own Rainbow Body. Feel how a circle of energy surrounding you can be full and hollow at the same time. Feel the force of it rising up until it becomes the pyramid of your own body. This is why in this mystical diagram the triangle rests upon two circles (Figure 48). This pyramid is at once the male generative organs, the symbol of pure Yang solar power, and the symbol of 9 Palaces Qi Gong. Embody this energy. Bring the symbol of circle, square, diamond, and point to your brow. Once you have felt this force, you have begun to build your immortal Rainbow Body. You have touched the essence of the cosmos and of your own self.

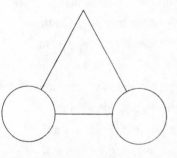

FIGURE 48

Ru Yi Gong is at once gentle, relaxing, and powerfully dynamic. Bringing opposite energies together for healing and growth is the hallmark of 9 Palaces Qi Gong. Continue swaying and visualizing for about five minutes, or until the waist feels warm, the body is very relaxed, and the hands tingle or feel thick or warm. Bring the hands up gently and place them over the mouth. Men put the right hand over the left, women, the left over the right. Visualize the color yellow. Feel this yellow Qi pouring from the palms into the mouth and down to the stomach. With the tongue on the roof of the mouth, its tip touching the soft palate, see if you can taste a flavor that starts off bitter or metallic and then turns sweet. If you can, it means your stomach and spleen channels are open. If not, you can start the swaying over again from the beginning until you do, but this is not necessary. Again, with practice, this channel will open up very quickly.

Most healthy people should be able to open the stomach and spleen channels without much difficulty. The spleen and stomach both digest and store water. Blockages can result in bloating and water retention. Muscle growth is related to the spleen and stomach. Muscle pain is also related to the spleen and stomach. Just sway and pump the spleen and stomach Qi up and down to help relieve these issues.

Basic Taoist dietary advice recommends eating less, only until you feel half-full. In the monastery, the monks would wake before dawn and drink large quantities of well water, as much as they could hold. After early-morning offices, a small breakfast of steamed buns and vegetables would be served. Another similar meal would be served no later than noon. After that, no other food would be available for the rest of the day other than perhaps a small bun in the afternoon if it was specially requested. Since the stomach and spleen are the "boss" organs, their function dictating all the other processes in the body, avoiding overeating removes a great potential strain on your system.

Other simple suggestions for a healthy stomach and spleen include avoiding becoming excited, moody, or angry. Remain calm, especially at meals. After each meal, it's advisable to walk one hundred steps, though heavy exercise or Qi Gong practice is best done before eating. Also, it is a good health practice to eat as many vegetables as possible. The Taoists believe the blood of animals contains toxic substances left over from their fright before being killed. However, strict vegetarianism is not mandatory in all Taoist sects. While Master Du was a vegetarian his entire life, Dr. Wu's Taoist "uncle," another master of advanced age he knew from his youth in the White Cloud Monastery, could be found eating meat on a regular basis. When Dr. Wu questioned him about this, he replied matter-of-factly that since animals suffered greatly in their last moments, he had taken it upon himself to eat of their flesh in order to assimilate and then release their souls with his Qi Gong practice. For the most part, Taoist medicine recognizes that people have different medical and dietary needs often based on their Chinese zodiac sign. For example, a person born in Year of the Tiger wouldn't feel right without having plenty of red meat, while a Sheep year person would do a lot better staying away from meat and eating a diet of leafy greens. Although this is a very detailed subject, the basic idea returns to the principle of *tong qi*, associating like with like.

To return to Ru Yi Gong, after you have tasted the sweet flavor in your mouth, finish by placing one palm on the stomach and one on the spleen, to the left and right of the actual location of the stomach. Feel the Qi going into the stomach and spleen, through to the innermost point. Hold the palms there until the organs feel very comfortable and calm. Along with the more esoteric aspects of Ru Yi Gong, simple stomach-related ailments, such as ulcers, bad breath, and even fever blisters (which result from excessive heat in the stomach), can be controlled with daily practice. Thus, one simple exercise becomes a prayer, a benediction, a positive affirmation, a health cure, an occult discipline, and a vehicle for building an immortal body.

Ru Yi Gong perfectly illustrates the paradox of Taoist cultivation, that so simple a movement can embody layer upon layer of powerful esoteric intent. Approach your practice based on what feels comfortable and simple to you. One never needs to struggle with the practice of Qi Gong. Cultivation is a pleasure and an honor and a responsibility, but not a struggle. If you can at one time assume the proud and exalted sense of self, feel the motion of rising and falling energy in the two vertical planes of the body, envision your body as a lotus flower, form the talisman of the Heavenly Eye, and finally propel yourself upward with the energy of the pyramid, you will not only have mastered this profound practice. You will have forever changed your powers of concentration and your body/mind connection.

SEVEN

The Fusion of Fire and Water

NOURISHING SKIN, NOSE, AND LUNGS

QI IS BREATH. There is no way to separate the function of breathing

from our interaction with Qi. Qi Gong enhances the body's intake of Qi in

large part by retraining the body to breathe. Why use the term *retrain*? The

evolution of the breathing process begins before birth. Inside the womb, babies breathe through their skin. Newborns and very young children naturally inhale through the nose and exhale through the mouth. As we get older, stress and anxiety can often cut us off from even the most basic rhythmic breathing. Disease is initially caused by lack of oxygen at least 65 percent of the time. Reoxygenating the body is fundamental to enhancing the immune system and promoting longevity. Whereas strenuous cardiovascular exercise can become harder on the body as we age, wiping out its benefits by adding excess strain to the rest of the system, Qi Gong refreshes the body's oxygen intake simply by returning to its earliest form. Practicing 9 Palaces Qi Gong promotes the balancing effect of breathing with nose and mouth, harmonizing Yin and Yang energies in the body. Besides developing equilibrium between inhalation and exhalation, it reopens the ability to breathe through our skin. This is Qi Gong. Once your skin is breathing, you can respond to the universe, to all of nature. Other forms of Qi Gong and martial arts teach external breathing practices, but nothing compares to the Taoist skin-breathing techniques. It's not unheard of for highly skilled Qi Gong practitioners to survive buried alive for up to ten days. They survive basically because they have perfected their ability to breathe through the skin. By learning how to breathe through the skin, we are regaining an important original ability from our earliest life.

The lungs represent heaven. They are an umbrella that forms a canopy above the organs. Once your skin can breathe again, you will see many aspects of life from a new perspective. Your ability to perceive and respond to the occurrences you encounter every day will be brought to a fresh level of insight. Every pore eliminates toxins, and every pore breathes and interchanges Qi with the universe. As you train your breathing with the next posture, your skin will naturally begin to reawaken and breathe freely again. You are tuning in to your heaven's messages.

From resting on the spleen and stomach, raise the hands up slowly facing the body, letting the arms rise up, of their own accord until they are above the head (Figure 49). The palms face downward, fingers pointing toward each other, ever so slightly forward from the center top of the head, or *ba hui* point. If you recall, the *ba hui* can be found at the intersection point of lines traced from the highest tips of the ears and the tip of the nose.

Not only is this a critical point for as the meeting point of the high concentration of Yang
channels in the head, as mentioned in Chapter
Five, it also serves as the exit point for your
internal light as it rises up to find your other
half.

Keep your hands aligned with each other by
feeling a current of energy between the middle
fingers. Hold until you feel a strong magnetic
field developing. Send columns of Qi from the
centers of the palms, through the *bai hui*, deep
into the brain. Rather than keeping the hands
directly above the *bai hui*, keep them just
slightly forward from this point when directing
the Qi. We're using the same principle as in
applying an acupuncture needle not directly
over a point but angled into the point from its
edge. This will more effectively open, stimulate,
and fill the *bai hui* with Qi. Alternately, you

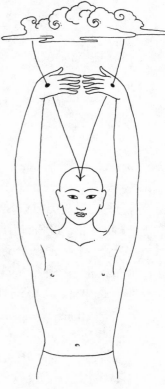

FIGURE 49

might prefer to spend the first forty-nine days of your practice sending
energy from the centers of the palms directly into the brain, without any particular focus on the *bai hui*. This is helpful to open up the general area first,
while you develop a better alignment between your fingertips. Once the *bai
hui* is thoroughly sensitized, its receptivity can be used to test the suitability
of different foods or medicines for yourself. Holding herbs or foods over this
point is a good example of how Taoist traditional energetic diagnosis works.
If the body's Qi has emerged, you can observe how it responds to coming in
contact with the material you are testing, either rejecting or responding to
the substance's properties.

As mentioned before, inhaling is related to the kidneys, exhaling to the
lungs. Though we will use another posture especially for unblocking the kidney meridian, we let breathing nourish and stabilize the brain with this exercise. Once in position, in the Heaven space above the eyebrows, visualize the
color white, or white clouds moving through the sky. Breathe in and out

through every pore of the skin. This might seem awkward at first, but let your mind go deep into the visualization and it will become easier.

With your hands still up in position, begin to smell a favorite smell, whatever you like best. Each person has a personal choice. Dr. Wu has used this concept to noticeable result in addition to his acupuncture and medical Qi Gong therapy. The Dragon Gate Classic refers to breast problems, cancer, tumors, and lumps under the skin as rocks. These are serious toxins within the body. This ancient text states that these growths occur when we are prevented from smelling the smells that we like for too long. Dr. Wu treated a patient with sixteen cysts in his chest area. Along with a course of acupuncture, medical Qi Gong, and herbs, the doctor presented him with sixteen bottles of different fragrances. He had the patient pick his favorite to take home with him to smell. Any time he thought of it, he would take out his bottle and smell the fragrance he chose. He now only has one cyst left, with minimal additional treatment. Don't be embarrassed to think about a fragrance you like all the time. If you're depressed, smell pleasant fragrances to uplift your mood. Some smells have particular healing properties. For example, the fragrance of fresh leaves is good for the heart.

As you smell your favorite aroma, breathe it into and out of every pore of the skin, along with the Qi and air. If you can spontaneously smell your favorite fragrance at this point in the practice, then you know you are replenishing yourself. Stand in this posture for one to two minutes, or until your body feels very light and starts to lift up. After the channel is opened, bring the hands down in loose fists to the sides of the nose, index fingers gently pressing into the points alongside the nostrils. This is the Sword Mudra. You'll be able to tell where these points are by a slight feeling of soreness or sensitivity. Place your finger swords on these points. While still visualizing the color white and smelling the fragrance, inhale through the nose slowly and thinly. Then exhale slowly, thinly, and silently through the mouth. With each inhale, breathe in Qi through every pore in the body and release it completely through each pore on the exhale. Repeat this breathing pattern nine times or more, until the body feels very clean and light. When you remove your fingers from next to the nostrils, the nose should feel tingling and light. Place the palms on the upper front of the chest, above the breasts.

Feel warm Qi going into the lungs, heating them through, until you feel very warm. See if you can taste a spicy, hot flavor in the mouth, and swallow it down to the lungs if it arrives.

There is a whole range of symptoms that can be balanced with this breathing balancing posture. Respiratory illness, colds, and stuffy nose can all be minimized and even prevented with daily practice of this posture. Western medicine maintains that colds and flu are caused by airborne bacteria and viruses, entering through the nose. Chinese medicine sees their cause from a different perspective. The lungs are connected to the pores. Colds are related to the lungs. They enter through pores. If the nose or sinuses are infected, the lungs are also infected. Treat the lung channels for nasal and sinus symptoms and use points around the nose to treat the lungs. Dry stool and constipation are also related to weak lungs. These complaints frequently beset older people due to lack of Qi. It's a must to replenish the lungs' Qi. Enhance the two-way function of the skin to enhance the lungs. The lung channel influences the entire body. The lungs affect hundreds of channels. Like a turtle in its shell, we can live longer and healthier lives by breathing through the skin.

There are also more esoteric practices associated with this lung posture. There is a secret Taoist ritual for wealth that utilizes this exercise. The lungs relate to the element of metal. In a private place where no one can see you, do the standing posture just described, imagining yourself surrounded on all sides by stacks of gold and jewels. Take extreme care that you are not observed. It's not recommended to use Qi Gong for base purposes, but this ritual is a valid traditional training to bring in money from questionable pursuits such as gambling or other shady sidelines. Just remember that any money you win at gambling, or even by playing the lottery, is considered by the Taoists as money stolen away from your future generations' inheritance. Proceed at your own risk.

On a lighter note, the Taoists also recount that within every pore of your body is an entire city, teeming with life going about its daily business just as we do. With today's electron microscopy, we certainly have photographic proof that many tiny organisms do indeed live in each pore. Were these the creatures the ancient Taoists were referring to? Maybe, maybe not. It's something fun to think about, at least.

LISTENING TO THE QI

QI SURROUNDS US. In the 9 Palaces, we are training ourselves to observe Qi using all of our faculties, heightening the five senses when needed to gain extra information and enrich our contact with the universe. This book has already discussed the many practices of training the eyes, both physical and Heavenly, to develop this interaction. Our eyes are important vessels of communication, both taking in and sending out messages to the world around us. Along with the sense of sight, the sense of hearing is extremely important for this communication. Before we are old enough to speak, we listen to the words spoken by our parents. We have to hear first before we can learn to respond with speech. Even when we are so young that we can barely keep our eyes open, we are listening to our new environment. In this sense, by training your hearing, you are developing one of the most fundamental aspects of your original abilities. The ears are related to the kidneys. If you have kidney problems, you probably don't hear well, either. The better you can hear, the better your kidney function. As the liver is the most important indicator of a woman's longevity, healthy kidneys are imperative for long life in men. Much has already been made about training the eyesight beyond its normal capacities to gain greater information from the world around us. With the next standing posture, we train our ears to listen to the Qi.

By purposefully extending one's hearing beyond its normal range, information on the internal workings of your body can be gleaned, not to mention messages and signs from the natural world outside the body. It's a natural function to be able to hear the sounds coming from inside the body. Everyone hears their stomach rumbling when they are hungry, for example. Fine-tuning this sense for more accurate troubleshooting is perhaps a lost art, but definitely not a skill that is beyond the reach of average persons willing to train themselves. With regular practice, you'll be surprised to find you are able to hear the water in your kidneys, the changes in the small intestines as they go through the digestion process, and many other important cues. In the monastery, the monks would practice to the point of hearing the words of scripture spoken character by character just by looking at the calligraphy on the scroll. They would write a word and then sit and listen to the sound of its Qi before going on to the next brushstroke. They also used their training for the protection of the monastery, as they could hear advancing gunshots and cannon fire from distances far beyond what the eye could see. Of course, this sensitivity was used in treating patients to "listen" to their health. Master Du was so skilled in his listening ability that he would know who would be waiting beyond the tall gates of the monastery each morning before they were unlocked and which supplicants were in the most desperate need of immediate attention.

Even today, this is a valid ability to develop, for treating patients, for protection, or just for a heightened awareness of the world around you. Certainly, there are many subtle signs and warnings we can learn to recognize all around us, when we know how to hear them. Just as our ears listen for sound, our whole body can listen to the Qi. Fill the body with Qi, and soon its messages will come in loud and clear.

To begin the practice, the arms and hands come out to the sides of the head, palms facing the ears. Be aware of your knees as very solid, a stable foundation for your stance. Visualize the color black as you feel a growing sense of magnetic attraction between your palms. You might even feel some sensations on your shoulders as well. Now start listening outwards for the sounds around you, out through the palms of the hands, then into the room, then past the building, out into the street and upward and outward as far as you can send your hearing (Figure 50). This is exactly the same process as in the eye/liver exercise. Every time the energy wants to contract back into the body, gently push it just a bit further out, all the way to the edge of the universe. Use your ears to search for the sounds of the Qi. Listen for the Qi, whatever personal meaning that takes on for you. After a minute or so, steadily bring the Qi back toward your ears. Keep pulling it back in until passes straight through the palms, through the skull, and out through the opposite sides, the two currents of Qi crossing as they pass through the head. This process should take from one and a half to two minutes total.

Afterward, nourish the kidneys and ears by bringing the palms of the

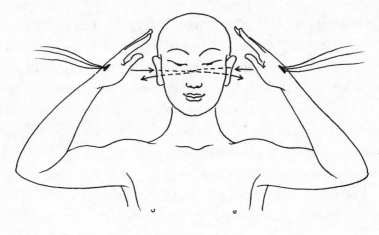

FIGURE 50

hands to the ears, the fingers resting on the back of the head. Perform three or nine ear suction presses just as in the warm-up exercises, continuing to visualize the color black. With this, you are purposely trying to enhance your ears' connection with your kidneys. It's important to stay as relaxed as possible while doing all these postures. While the left brain controls conscious thought, subconscious awareness of your training is being continuously stored in the right hemisphere as you practice. The more relaxed you become, the more information your right brain will remember from your Qi Gong efforts. Practicing 9 Palaces Qi Gong helps make the connections and imprints new neural pathways between the right brain and the left. The right brain has so much underdeveloped potential. The Taoists have been charting these waters for thousands of years. Today we have the chance to bring the results of their study into our daily lives.

THE SWALLOW

JUST AS AN experienced mechanic can diagnose what is wrong with a car by listening to the sounds it makes, we can learn to listen to the messages being carried to us on the currents of Qi. A constant flow of information steadily surrounds us as we move through our day. The practice of 9 Palaces

Qi Gong helps us to attune to this endless flow by augmenting our basic ability to see, taste, smell, and hear. A Taoist understands that Qi can be touched and felt in other, more subtle ways as well.

After awakening all the other organs' connection with the universal Qi, we now come to the heart. The heart can be our greatest ally in our ongoing communication with the flow of Qi. A strong foundation of balance throughout the body is best developed to aid our heart's energy in its attempts to reach out to external Qi. As the interplay of fire and water, heart and kidneys, is crucial to this communication, we must lead into the heart practice by first neutralizing any weakness left in the kidneys.

As we've already learned, how do we best regulate our kidneys? By just working on our ears. Chinese medicine relates high blood pressure and the feeling of light-headedness associated with it to problems with the kidneys. A light-headed sensation can indicate that the kidneys are weak and need rebalancing. After doing the three to nine ear suction presses that finish the last set, squeeze and pinch the cartilage at the back of the ears between the fingers and thumbs (Figure 51). You can grab onto the entire stalk of flesh connecting the ear to the head with all the fingers plus the thumb, or just concentrate on the tiny flap of skin right at the center of this stalk with forefinger and thumb. Concentrate on squeezing out any imbalances. Pinch this area from nine to one hundred times, until the body feels regulated and balanced. This lowers or raises the blood pressure as needed.

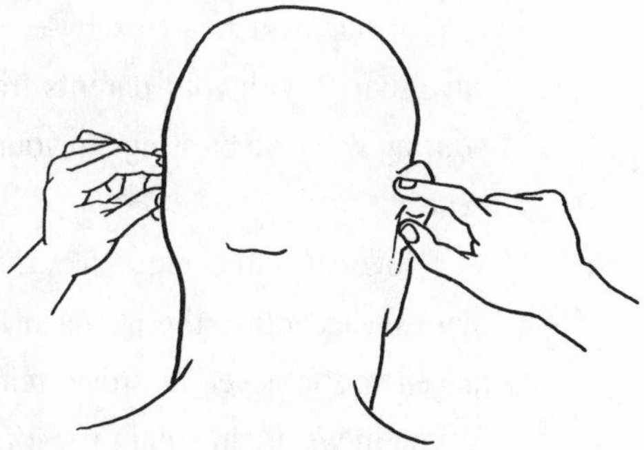

Though it's a simple massage over a seemingly small and overlooked part of the body, don't be mistaken.

FIGURE 51

Squeezing the back of the ears is highly effective. It can very significantly regulate your blood pressure. You can test the benefits of this massage with as little as twenty-seven pinches between two blood pressure readings. If you are a doctor and have high-blood-pressure patients, teach them to do this. It will positively augment any other treatment they are receiving. This massage also helps balance the brain and the nerves within the brain. If you're tired, the ear pinching will wake up your brain.

The heart is governed by the southern direction. Generally birds fly to the south, and the Animal Lord of the south is the Red Bird. Therefore, with our next posture we will need to think of ourselves as a bird. Doing this is not only good for your heart; it can enhance the health of your parents. It doesn't work for siblings or spouses, but for your mother and father, it is a wonderful way of bringing them longevity from your Qi Gong practice. We all should be very thankful to our parents for bringing us into the world and caring for us when we were at our most helpless and needy. With the swallow posture we give them our best blessings, even if they are not nearby, or no longer alive.

How do you help others who are not with you, simply through a standing posture or breathing technique? This is the Taoist principle of *Dong Ta Xin Chu*, or "Going Through From One's Heart." It's a way of communicating with others, sending them out an energetic message from inside one's body. When you have already developed a bond with another, it lives inside both of you and can be brought out to contact each other. Just as the Red Bird is a heavenly messenger, bringing fortunate tidings where he flies, the swallow posture of our next heart exercise releases the messages of love and care you have shared with your parents from the day of your birth. This natural outpouring will give blessings to your parents, wishing them longevity and good health.

How can a technique like this possibly work? Certainly, there is an element of accepting the power of positive suggestion behind this theory. On an energetic level, positive reinforcement can have a dramatic effect. Although we are in still in the infancy of researching this scientifically, there still are ways to test the concept. There have been studies showing that exposing plants to loud, dissonant music will stunt their growth, while gentle, harmonious music will encourage them. Talking to your plants, encouraging them to grow as you water them, is a perfect example of loving communication reaching out to life forms seemingly incapable of cognition.

Of course, the Taoists have had many opportunities to study these impalpable concepts. In the world of the monastery, the Tao brothers would travel from school to school, always conducting their business in person. If a monk had to leave the monastery on a journey, a pot of flowers or a plant would be put out for him in his name. The master would study the plant every day to see how his student was faring. If suddenly one day one leaf dropped, the master would call for another monk to hurry and catch up with his brother, to help him with the trouble that had befallen him.

This is something Dr. Wu has done with his own students. Sometimes the student would give him a plant, designating it as his representation while he or she would be away. Sometimes Dr. Wu would pick a plant or flower and have his student or patient touch it or water it before he or she went away. Even this would be enough to create the bond, as long as both people had put their thoughts into it. Dr. Wu feels this method is quite accurate, after testing it many times.

In the same way, certain Qi Gong techniques can reach out and help your parents, enhancing their health and longevity. Sometimes you will be able to sense things in your fingers. As we spoke of before, if anything goes wrong with your first finger, something is happening to your mother. The middle finger relates to your father. Recall the patient who burned her own favorite dress to help her mother, after feeling the sharp signal of pain in her finger. Her mother was on the other side, but she still needed something. There really is no scientific way to analyze this. It is part of the Tao. These are matters of the Six Realms. The studies of the Tibetan lamas are very accurate regarding the realms after death, but the earliest records derive from Taoist artifacts.

After pinching the backs of the ears, we now move to the Swallow Posture. The hands come slowly down, palms down and to the back, palms tilted up. At this point it is preferable to be facing the sun. Facing the sun and also facing south at the same time is best. As mentioned before, the heart is related to the southern direction, which also represents the summer season and the element of Fire. If you are facing south, your fingers will be pointing northeast and northwest once they are behind you. The arms are pulled all the way to the back, pinching the shoulder blades together as much as possible and lifting and thrusting out the rib cage. (Figure 52.) Feel your middle fingers growing out as long as they can. The chin is tucked firmly into the neck. The stomach is drawn in but held without tension, to more

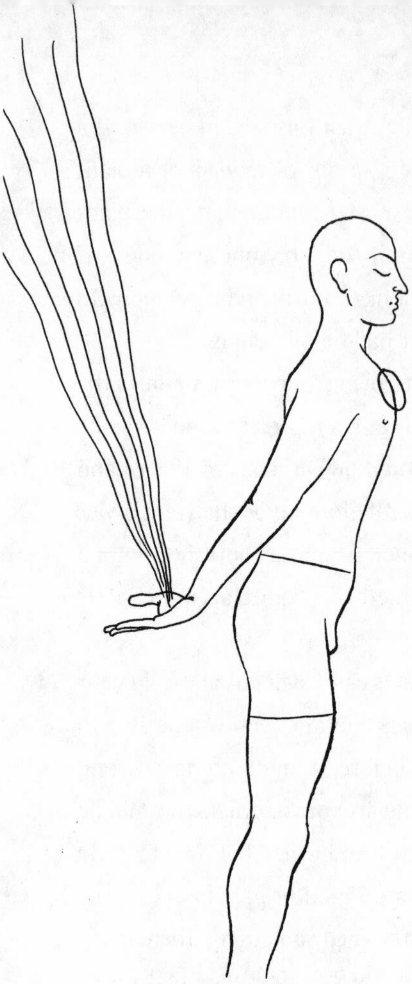

FIGURE 52

completely emphasize the stretch through the rib cage. See and feel your posture as it relates to a bird sitting with its breast out and its wings folded back, taking in the sun.

In Chinese medicine, the heart is considered the emperor, governing the function of the rest of the body. If the emperor cannot see clearly, then the other organs are in danger. The heart is able to think. In English, the eyes are portrayed as the "windows of the heart." This holds true in Chinese thought, which also believes you can see a person's true feelings through the eyes. Taoist medicine takes this one step further and sees the heart as also having eyes, to see the workings of the organs as well as to send out the emotions. This is the sense in which the Heart Practice is related to the mind. When the heart feels twisted or blocked, there is a direct correlation to the thoughts passing through the mind. During major sporting events, the hospitals are always busy. If your heart is weak, don't let yourself get excited or overstimulated.

Standing in the Swallow Posture exposes the two Yang channels on the front of the body, which comprises the stomach channel. As the heart relates to the emotions and is the governor of all the organs, so it is related to the stomach, which also plays a great role in the connection between the emotions and the body's general health and is associated with the central direction and the element of Earth. Earth is important to us. It affects us in many areas. The point between the thumb and index finger, which you can locate by pressing and finding the spot that feels sore, treats the stomach and diaphragm. If you have a stomachache, cover your mouth, as after the stomach-swaying posture. This will also help with menstrual pain. The Swallow Posture will harmonize the relationship between the heart and the stomach. It also helps the heart and liver in their shared supervision of the eyes.

When standing in the Swallow Posture, the tip of the tongue is on the upper palate, joining the Ren and Du channels, which when connected form the Microcosmic Orbit. While the mouth corresponds to the stomach, the tongue and the heart reflect each other. As a result, in Taoist medicine, food remedies are generally recommended to treat conditions based on the diagnosis of the tongue. For tongue analysis, look at your tongue in the mirror first thing in the morning when you wake up. A light-textured, pale white tongue is healthy. If you didn't sleep well, the tongue will be swollen. If you feel tired or sore, you will see teeth imprints on the sides of the tongue. If you have a toothache, your tongue will be red.

If only the tip of the tongue is red, your heart is on fire. Eating plenty of watermelon will cool it, which also helps calm hot-tempered, angry people or conditions where the face becomes flushed and red. Besides watermelon, bitter foods also help cool down the heart. If the saliva is sticky, eat foods that dissolve mucus, such as apples or oranges in particular.

From a Western as well as a Chinese perspective, a small glass of red wine before bed is also good for the heart. Conversely, hot, spicy foods can be difficult on the heart, leading to moodiness. In particular, to keep the spleen regulated, avoid very cold as well as highly spiced food. Keeping a diet moderated between heating and cooling foods is key to balance between stomach and heart. Beans are very powerful healing foods. Mixed bean soup is a strong healing elixir. Boil the beans and then drink the strained broth. Green beans, such as mung beans, are good for the liver, ridding it of blockages. When the liver Qi rises and there is too much heat, green food will lower this unwanted heat. Different-colored beans also enhance body functions. Red beans enhance the heart. Yellow beans reduce fatigue. Black beans enhance the kidneys. After an animal or human gives birth, feed them black beans. The world is whole in its unity. We are all together, animals, plants, and humans as one with the Five Elements. This is the subtle philosophy behind Taoist medicine, moving away from herbs and concentrating on the harmonies of food and Qi Gong to heal all in need.

Though there is a tendency to do so, make sure not to hold your breath in the Swallow Posture. For the first forty-nine days of practice, you can simply stand in this position breathing gently and naturally for three minutes, keeping the whole body relaxed even while keeping the chest elevated and the shoulders pinched together. Use the sensation of the middle fingers growing long to keep your posture aligned and the energy balanced as it circulates. At the next level of practice, while trying to keep your chest as elevated as possible without tensing up, inhale in a quick sniff through the nose and exhale in two quick, even bursts—HA! HA!—through the mouth. The sniff through the nose should be relatively soundless and relaxed but full and deep enough to shoot through the nasal passages, fill the head, and cycle down into the chest, where it is instantly released with the two "HA"s. Each "HA" should feel gently explosive, involving the chest as well as the mouth. Repeat this breathing pattern nine times, or until the chest is warm. The warmth signifies the Qi of the heart coming out. This is another good example of how Qi Gong uses breathing combined with subtle stretches to massage and release tension from the innermost layers of muscle, bone, and connective tissue out. Alternately, instead of this special breathing pattern, you can just breathe naturally while in the Swallow Posture, until the chest feels warm.

If you find it difficult to stay in this posture or you have trouble keeping your arms back and out and your shoulder blades pinched tightly together, keep the principle of kong, or emptiness, in mind. Instead of straining with how well you are stretching and expanding yourself into the posture, focus on the empty, hollow, rounded space inside your rib cage, ready to be filled with sun and breath. You will find that your body will readily relax deeper into the stretch and you will get more out of the breathing pattern. Over time, three minutes a day standing in the Swallow Posture will correct many crucial posture points along the back, while acting as a "balloon" for the rib cage, helping to clear arterial blockages in the heart brought on by years of poor posture.

With practice, concentration, and sincerity, you may feel an outpouring of energy from your heart during the Swallow Posture. This is the point where your inner heartfelt hopes for your parents will come out. There is no need to actively think of prayers or loving wishes. Just imagine yourself transformed into a bird, and feel your chest opening up and your heart expanding, filling and releasing. You are making the effort to open yourself physically. With a sincere heart, all your best blessings will come out on their own. This is the essence of "Going Through From One's Heart."

While still in the Swallow Posture, lightly clench the teeth and run the tip of the tongue in a clockwise circle around the inner surface of the teeth nine times (Figure 53). Men can begin this clockwise circling from the left side of the mouth over to the right and then around. Women should start from the right and move left. Make sure to contact the backs of the upper and lower teeth. The point is to stimulate saliva. Swallow the accumulated saliva all the way down to the lower *dan tian*. Repeat these two steps of breathing nine times then circling the tongue and swallowing the saliva one to three times or, preferably, nine times for complete results.

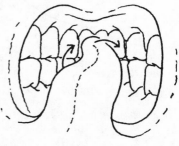

FIGURE 53

Yet again, a very powerful practice comes to the student of Qi Gong in a surprisingly simple form. Accumulating and swallowing saliva in this manner is in fact one of the fundamental operations of *nei dan*, the inner *dan*. While other aspects of 9 Palaces Qi Gong are involved with clearing the body and communicating with the universe, *nei dan* is what could most easily be described as internal alchemy, transforming substances within the body for purification and creation of new energies, most frequently the saliva. *Nei dan* practices are often the final step in the preparatory stages before beginning the central portion of 9 Palaces or 5 Centers Qi Gong. While standing in the Swallow Posture, collecting the saliva is called *Jin Jing Yu Yeon*, "Refining the Golden Jade Elixir." You have specially prepared your saliva to be swallowed down to the lower *dan tian* as a medicine. It has the ability to enhance one's health and prevent disease, helping the body to fight off infections and

FIGURE 54

fatigue and easing stomach problems. For older people who might be having trouble swallowing their food, doing this practice can bring positive results in as little as a week's time.

Don't we naturally swallow our saliva all the time? Although saliva does have some natural antiseptic qualities, it is the posture and especially the rotation of the tongue around the teeth that "charges" a fluid we already produce into a more powerful substance than its basic form. This is the essence of *nei dan*. Specific body postures and motions change our brain function and our state of mind and, as a result, our body chemistry. The Taoists have studied these subtle differences for thousands of years. Today, encephalograms show scientifically the differences in brain function when a subject is sitting, standing, or lying down, eyes open or shut, and so on. By standing in the Swallow Posture and rotating your tongue, you will change the quality of your saliva. Dr. Wu tested this out by trying to generate saliva while in many different positions. Only in this position did the flavor of his saliva change, becoming saltier. The Taoist scholars would test every type of daily behavior to see if one position over another would bring a greater health benefit. Even sleeping was tested, discovering that while sleeping lying down was indeed the best position for aiding the immune system, sleeping standing up or even hanging upside down could help the practitioner to focus his or her energy in specialized ways. Test it for yourself and see. The key point is to rotate the tongue no less than nine times.

Finish by bringing the hands up and together in a prayer posture at a level between the heart and the brow (Figure 54). From spending some time with this practice, you will perceive how each step absorbs, focuses, and then nourishes energy precisely into the heart center, deeper and deeper until you reach its core. The effortlessness, gentleness, and naturalness with which you practice are the only tools needed to send out the kind thoughts and blessings you have within your soul.

E I G H T

Chrysalis

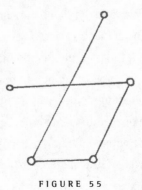

FIGURE 55

THE SUN IS the heart of the universe. It pumps life into every living

thing. Passing from movement to movement, breath to breath, your prac-

tice takes flight, a mystical journey to the center of the sun. The 9 Palaces

Qi Gong training gives birth to a vast range of physical, emotional, and

spiritual reflections and responses. You are free to take on any role you

choose as you voyage to the outer reaches of the cosmos and the innermost spaces of heart and mind. Use your 9 Palaces practice as a time to express your feelings of gratitude to those who have helped you, your love for the beauty of the natural world, and your respect and worship of your god and your ancestors. It's all totally up to you. The exercises are so simple and profound, they lay before you as a blank slate on which to write your deepest feelings about being alive.

Especially as we begin the last segment of the 9 Palaces Qi Gong, leave any doubts or worries about seeing results behind. Forget the mundane tasks you spend the rest of the day laboring over. Just as a dancer conjures all her grace and oneness with the music as she leaps onstage, just as a musician draws the bow across his violin, the sounds he hears in his mind even sweeter than the notes he coaxes from his instrument—now is your time to give voice to your unique message to the universe. The more you can approach the practice of Qi Gong as an art form that allows you to speak of your truest feelings, the closer you will come to embodying the wisdom that thousands of years of sages, scholars, and saints sought so hard to preserve.

This final section is the actual 9 Palaces form as preserved in the sacred texts of the Dragon Gate Sect. While the first sections warmed and unlocked your body to the universal Qi, they were but a preparation for this moment. Now it is time to use the energies you have gathered and the channels of communication you have opened to create a new energy. The pyramid is the symbol of the refined life force. Pure Yang, it is potent enough to thrust beyond the energetic level of the material plane into the realm of the Rainbow. As the other great symbol of the 9 Palaces Qi Gong, this diagram is the key to letting this mighty force find its proper path for release (Figure 55).

If you look carefully, you will see it is a pathway superimposed upon the pentagram of the Five Elements. Instead of the usual star, it plots a course from the green sphere of the liver to the yellow sphere of the spleen, down to the white of the lungs, the black of the kidneys and then finally up through the red sphere of the heart and beyond. It is a map of the course the energy generated by 9 Palaces practice takes within the body. Think back to the order of the postures of the second section. We started with the eye/liver posture, opening a line of communication from the body out to the farthest reaches of the universe and then back to the deepest point within the micro-

cosm of the liver. Then came the spleen/stomach, lung, kidney, and heart postures. You are drawing this diagram with the energies of the senses and
organs, unblocking, balancing, and nourishing each one in sequence. With
the final section of the 9 Palaces form, you will draw these five Qis, wood,
earth, metal, water, and fire, into a protective shell, formed with the sun;
then prepare their final cleansing with the light and heat of the sun, and at
last release all that you have built in a final flash. You have unleashed a new
force strong enough to cut through all bonds and limitations, a new power
explosive enough to shoot past the boundaries of the limited world we live
in and make contact with the cosmic. Just as you opened communication
individually between each organ and the universal Qi, combined, you have
liberated a channel from your innermost being to the sun, father energy of
the universe and the source of all life.

Begin by bringing the hands from behind you as they were held in the
Swallow Posture, up in a prayer position. Your hands should be about two
fists' distance from your chest between heart and eye level. Your two palms
together symbolize the merging of Yin and Yang. Feel a connection between
your browline and the tips of your fingers. Pause for a moment to feel the
halves of your body uniting, flowing, calming, unifying. Be of one heart and
one mind. From this point on, there should be no talking or interruption until
the completion of the form.

The prayer posture is a very powerful centering position. Never tell a lie
while standing in prayer posture. You will bring harm to yourself. Settle your
body and mind by imagining yourself standing at the bottom of the sea.
Though the surface of the ocean may be boiling with currents and agitated
with tall waves, float downward into its depths to experience the perfect
silence of its sandy floor. A hurricane's eye is calm. Feel its stillness. The right
hand is Yin and the left hand is Yang. Join your hands together and your
focus will naturally arise.

After you begin to feel calm, there is one more step to take to release
yourself into a state of complete serenity before continuing on. While still
standing in the prayer posture, recite this small but critical mantra: "*Bu tan
cai, bu xi ming*" (pronunciation: *Boo tan tsai, boo shee ming*): "I am not
greedy for wealth, I am not afraid of death" is the most literal translation of

this phrase. However, it takes a broader understanding to grasp this mantra's full implications. We have to look beyond the things that limit us in this life. Fear and greed are the most powerful forces that hold us back as we struggle on the spiritual path. We fear death so deeply and subconsciously that it pervades the choices we make day in and day out. Without realizing we are being guided by fear of sickness and death, we avoid risks and confuse our objectivity when confronted with forces or events outside our comfort zone. Thus we pass up opportunities to grow.

We also create limitations in our lives when we covet the things that others have. That money and fame cannot ensure complete security is only part of greed's danger. By always struggling to achieve an outcome that is based on an outside, generalized standard, we take ourselves further and further away from the knowledge of what is good for us individually. We each come into this world with unique opportunities and capabilities. The Qi Gong practitioner must internalize the realization that to uncover one's True Self, all that does not come from the self must be seen for its transitory and illusory nature. To strip away this excess weight requires courage, the conviction that what is real will remain, even as everything else falls away.

Bu tan cai: No worries, greed or excess. *Bu xi ming*: No fear of death, no fear of sickness, nothing can do you harm. Speak these two phrases for purification. Once you are far from worry and greed, you can make great strides in your cultivation. If you are not afraid to die, what else can trouble you? Evil forces cannot attach themselves to a strong body. A resolute spirit is the foundation of a strong body. As you embody the spirit of *Bu tan cai, bu xi ming,* you become impossible to defeat.

As part of his "reeducation" during the Cultural Revolution, Dr. Wu was sent to do forced labor in a coal mine. The excavation in progress touched off a landslide. Huge gouts of dirt and rock collapsed and were heading toward the workers, who had nowhere to run. Dr. Wu calmly sat down in the lotus position with his hands in a prayer mudra, thought of his teacher, and repeated this mantra over and over again as he and seven other nearby workers were buried alive. Out of the eight, Dr. Wu was the only one to survive.

Bu tan cai, bu xi ming: I am not greedy for things that are not mine to have; I am not afraid of death, sickness and evil cannot attack. Repeat this mantra nine times or more. It can be said aloud or to oneself, in Chinese or English, slowly or run together quickly—whatever is most meaningful and heartfelt. You will know what's right for you. When you feel your consciousness change, you will know that your prayer has succeeded. Remember that God is in the heart and in the workings of the universe, not statues or paintings. The True God lives within heaven and the heart. True prayer occurs between the heart and heaven. Your parents too are an embodiment of God. Think of them, and that which is God will strengthen your heart.

WORSHIPPING THE SUN

STILL IN PRAYER position, the hands pull down the center of the body, to the lower *dan tian*, where they separate and open, palms down. Continuing the motion, the hands circle upward, the palms flipping up as the arms open. Inhale through the nose in a gentle, continuous stream as the hands circle up in a wide circle. Still inhaling, the hands meet together in the prayer position over the head, at top of the circle, like a steeple or lightning rod. Then pull down slowly, bringing down Heavenly Qi as you continue to inhale. (Figure 56.) Once you reach the Heart Center, begin your second circle by continuing pulling down back to the lower *dan tian*, exhaling through the mouth. Separate and open the palms again as before and continue. Make a total of four grand circles, ending the last one in the prayer position at heart level. If it is too difficult to continuously inhale through the nose as you form the circle and pull down into the body, it is better to breathe naturally as your arms go up and just inhale as you pull down the Heavenly Qi.

Make sure you make exactly four circles, not one less or one more. This is your opening prayer to the sun. Whereas in the first two sections of the 9 Palaces, you can do your warm-ups as many times as you need to open and unblock the flow of Qi, in this last section, certain numbers of repeats are intrinsic to the motions, for they act together numerologically as esoteric communication with the sun. Four circles here is your signal to the sun that you are beginning your practice. The sphere of energy that you and the sun create together with this motion is your sacred space for the rest of the form.

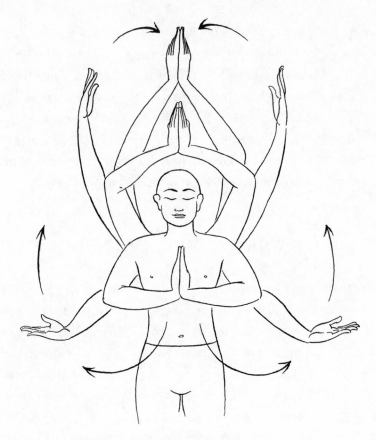

FIGURE 56

Tibetan Buddhists also worship the sun using this same exercise. The only difference is that after they are finished, they lie down. As the 9 Palaces' purpose is not only to gather energy from the sun, but to open a pathway of communication with it, we continue from here.

SPINNING THE COCOON

AFTER VENERATING THE sun with four wide circles, more circles are going to be made. However, these circles will have a different energetic purpose, one that is crucial to gaining the great benefits the 9 Palaces Qi Gong has to offer. Palms still together in prayer position at heart level, elbows bent,

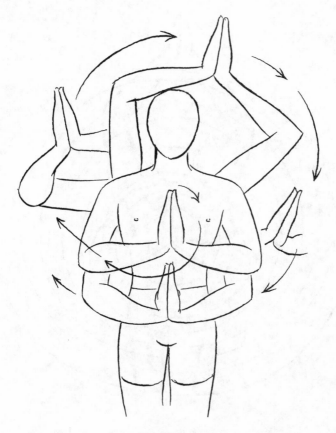

FIGURE 57

start moving them in a circular pattern. Use a clockwise motion, where the arc of the circle swings from center top downward on the left and up on the right to end again at center top (Figure 57). Keep the wrists gentle and loose. Remember, the joints are storage points for Qi. By keeping your elbows and wrists loose while you circle, you will increase the flow of Qi within your movement. Feel your energy flowing upward and outward as your circles grow in diameter. Circle in increasingly large circles, but without dipping your elbows below heart level, until the peak of the circles reach above head. Make exactly 9 circles, ending with the hands over the top of the head. (Figure 58.)

Pause slightly at the top of your ninth circle, then return back in a counterclockwise motion exactly six times, decreasing the size of the circle on

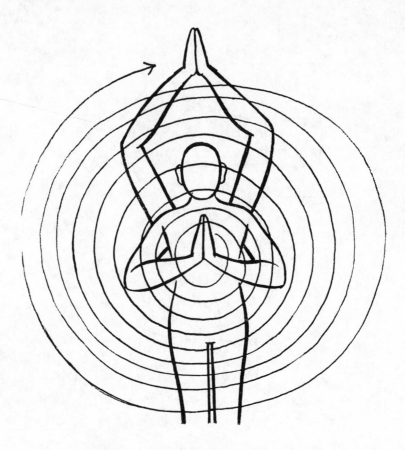

each revolution (Figure 59). Feel the expansive Yang energy you created with your outward growing circles flowing back in as your Yin circles become smaller. Your last circle should be so small that its movement is almost imperceptible and yet you feel its energy gently pouring inward, suffusing you. Your sixth Yin circle should end with your arms held right above heart level. Breathe gently and naturally throughout. There is no special inhalation or exhalation involved. Keep your shoulders, neck, arms, and wrists loose throughout and your circling motion supple and fluid.

The crucial point to remember here is that when you are building your clockwise outward circles, you must make exactly nine of them. These are Yang circles: energizing, generating, forward-moving energy. The returning, diminishing circles are Yin. You must do six of them, again not one more or

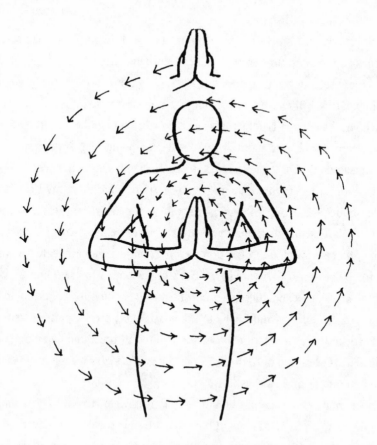

FIGURE 59

one less. Their energy is pulling inward, penetrating and nourishing. When you are drawing your circles, count how many you have made under your breath, so that you don't accidentally make the wrong count. There is a special relationship between the numbers 9 and 6. First 9, then 6, from big to small. It is a signal to the universe.

We all use nonverbal signals in everyday life. For example, Chinese manners require one not to embarrass one's guests by asking them to leave. If it is time to end their visit, it is customary to raise your teacup just so. It would be considered terribly impolite to say you are too busy or you have somewhere else to be. Just lift your teacup and your guest will know it's time to be off. The same thing applies if you are the guest. If you bring tea or something else to drink to your host, you are implying that you have other things to do afterward. Your host will recognize the gesture and will make sure to lift his cup in good time so that you can politely leave.

Every society has its own social rules. They aren't secrets, but if you are unfamiliar with them, they can seem like a mysterious, unfathomable code. Once you have been taught the proper signals, you will be able to relate to them comfortably and naturally; 9 and 6, expanding and contracting, work in this same way. These movements are the Heavenly codes. They contain specific information used to communicate certain energies. A mystical Taoist epigram begins, "Heaven One created water—Nine completes it." In the Tao, 9 is the largest number. For the energy we are creating with 9 Palaces Qi Gong, there is specific information we are trying to communicate outwards to the universe. So there are specific reasons we need to use 9 and 6 in our motions, just as we practice starting with the liver, going to the spleen, to the lungs, to the kidneys, and finally to the heart. It is a precise pattern from the *I Ching*, designed for a particular effect. If you visit the Zhongnan mountains, you will see it carved onto the ancient tablets of Lao Zi's teachings. These are the inner maps of 9 Palaces Qi Gong.

The number 9 is Yang; the number 6 is Yin. There are natural rhythms in the universe. In temples across China and Tibet, you will find prayer wheels turning. The Earth rotates around its axis just as the prayer wheels turn. Tibetan Buddhists practice this turning motion with prayer wheels. It can also be practiced within the body itself. This turning relieves others of spiritual bondage, as well as oneself. Silkworms turn with the same motion as they wrap themselves with silk. After they have spun their cocoons, they will emerge later, beautiful and light of wing. The circling of 9 and 6 is our inner prayer wheel, our own chrysalis spinning. You have to be exact. It must be nine clockwise Yang outward and six counterclockwise Yin inward. Some movements in 9 Palaces Qi Gong can be done nine times or a little more, but this particular movement has to be precisely nine and six. By following this count, your body will experience a special reaction from it automatically. The silkworm spins its new home by turning just so. The texts of the Dragon Gate Classic observe that the larva spits its silk out nine times in one direction and then six in the other as it builds its casing. It wraps itself inside and quietly begins to change, protected from any outside interference. Once it has transformed itself, it must chew a hole in its tiny silken ball. Then it can at last burst forth in flight. The 9 Palaces Microcosmic Orbit Qi Gong lets you become the silkworm. You are the silkworm spinning its safe haven; you are inside your cocoon, gestating your new abilities; and eventually you will be able to fly out.

Our souls desire their flight. We yearn to free ourselves. This is the spiritual journey that the 9 Solar Palaces practice sets us upon. We open, purify, and energize the organs and senses that are our tools for communicating with the universe. This is the secret of the Rainbow Body. The flight of the Rainbow Body to take on its cosmic role in the heavens is the ultimate goal of 9 Palaces Qi Gong. We create the cocoon from our natural energies and we fly out from it using their force again, transformed. To release its inner light is each spirit's deepest craving. Finding this freedom is very important. You could say you have no interest in attaining a Rainbow Body. Why should you bother remembering the 9 and the 6 exactly? You don't have to set the Rainbow Body as your goal, but even without that desire, the 9 and 6 circles will bring your personal abilities out. You will raise your level, just as if you were turning a prayer wheel.

Of course, there is no guarantee that you will accomplish the ultimate feat of the Rainbow Body, but at least you can become a beautiful butterfly. Don't ever doubt it. Don't question if it is really working. As soon as you let doubts enter your mind, you will be automatically rejecting the full potential of the 9 Palaces. As the martial artist must never aim to hit his opponent, but instead focus on punching the wall behind him to inflict maximum force, you need to allow faith its space in your practice. With conviction and continuous practice for one to three months, you will feel the change, especially in the clarity of your Heavenly Eye. You have to practice very well, with sincerity. See if you can open it.

Sometimes if even with serious practice you have difficulty opening your Heavenly Eye, it's possible you don't have the natural ability to open it, or you may need to practice further. Dr. Wu believes that with consistent and sincere practice, most people should be able to open their Heavenly Eye in one hundred days. Afterward, you are going to see new things all around you. Don't worry about the results. If you start slowly and are disciplined about

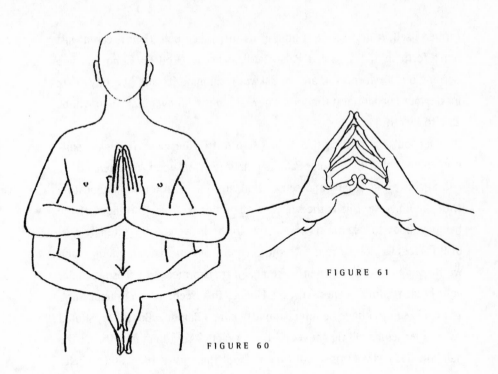

FIGURE 61

FIGURE 60

daily practice, it will come. You will lift your own personal level of potential higher by doing the practice. Then you will not only understand your surroundings and environment in a new light, but there are other influences that will become clear to you as well. Each person's talents are different; no two experiences will be the same. But as varied as we may be, there are an equal number of forces helping us and coexisting with us, waiting to be found. There's no secret to it. Just practice 9 Palaces for a period of time, and you will feel it. As you open your Heavenly Eye, you will have a more advanced understanding of this practice. Many of the things discussed in these pages will seem much clearer. There is much wonder to be discovered when your soul's light is free to explore its true domain.

After you have completed the circling, the hands are still in prayer position, palms together at heart level. As we've said, the 9 and 6 circling is a signal to the universe. The posture the hands are held in while circling further defines this sign. Circling with palms pressed together is the proclamation of belief in one's God. You are announcing your faith to the cosmos. Practice

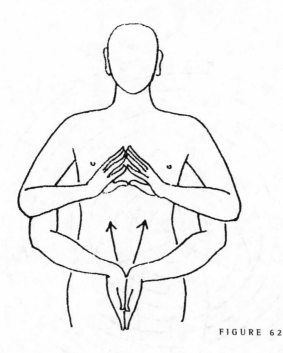

FIGURE 62

with sincerity. There is no one right perception of the God force. There is no need to invoke or visualize Buddha or Lao Zi or Jesus or Gaia. Feeling a sense of integration between pure movement and pure devotion is the key. As you finish your last inward circle, while still in prayer position at heart level, flip your hands downward from the wrists (Figure 60). With the palms still together pointing downward, push down the center of the body from heart level to below the lower *dan tian*, until the arms are fully extended. With an even movement, separate your palms while still keeping the fingertips pressed together (Figures 61–62), and bring your arms back up to heart level in a smooth, rounded arc (Figure 62).

Now circle nine times outward and six times inward just as before, with the fingertips together in their steeplelike posture (Figure 63). Circling clockwise outward, ending overhead in this mudra, you are now making contact with your ancestors. Because you have contacted them with sincere belief, as you circle counterclockwise back inward, you are bringing back the messages they have been waiting to give you (Figure 64). Again, you don't need to pic-

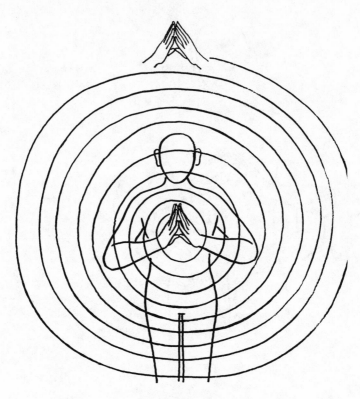

FIGURE 63

ture their faces in your mind. What your family heritage holds for you will be retrieved naturally within this rotating hand seal.

After returning to heart level, the hands flip down from the wrists while still in fingertips-together posture and again push down past the lower *dan tian* (Figure 65). Gracefully clasp the hands together, fingers gently but firmly interlaced in the final hand seal (Figure 66). The clasped hands turn up in an arc, ending at heart level (Figure 67), and begin the nine clockwise circles outward. This time, instead of keeping the size of your circles contained to the area between the heart and the arms' extension overhead, make the circle grow as large as you can without locking the elbows. After its diameter reaches a certain size at about the fourth or fifth circle, start slightly opening the palms with the fingers still interlaced as the hands descend below heart level, clasping them again as they rise above heart level, as if with each

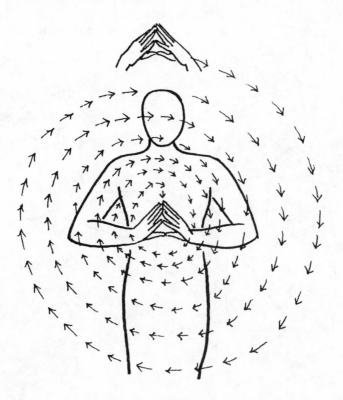

FIGURE 64

opening in the cycle you are releasing heavenly Qi to the Earth and with each closing pulling up the Earth's Qi, clasping to reunite it with the heavenly Qi overhead. The wider the arc of your circle, the wider you should open your palms, your momentum carrying through more Qi with each revolution. End with hands clasped overhead in a momentary pause (Figure 68). Just as the previous hand seal makes contact with your ancestors, the final hand seal makes contact with the god you believe in. If you do not believe in a traditional God, you can take this moment to connect with the knowledge of your highest self. While the first hand seal announced your belief in this source of all things, the final hand seal allows you to commune with it and come back with its wisdom and guidance.

When finishing your six decreasing circles, again open the palms to the earth in the larger circles. In the smallest circles, the hands remain clasped.

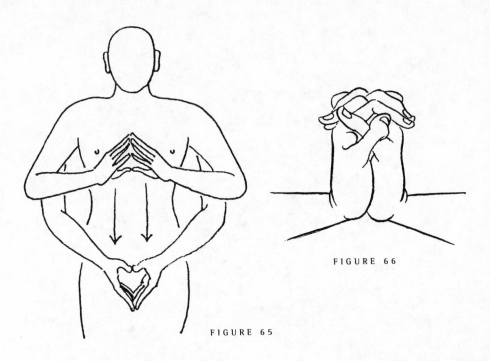

FIGURE 66

FIGURE 65

End at heart level with the hands clasped (Figure 69). At this point, you have spun your precious cocoon. The three hand seals bring us the messages of the Three Realms. The first seal is Human. You are making a personal proclamation to the All. It is your voice, the statement of your heart's belief. The second seal is Heaven. You are communicating with the Ling Qi, the heavenly messages of the spirit realms, bringing back the gifts of the ancestors. The third seal is Earth. Refining the Earth energy you draw into yourself, you stand in the balance between Earth and Heaven, ready to accept the messages of God. Use what appears to you now to make wise choices for your life. The wisdom you have contacted with your practice of these seals will help you make the best decisions for yourself.

The nine clockwise rotations and six counterclockwise rotations comprise a basic universal pattern of energy, mirrored all around us. This vortex of energy can be found in all three realms, Human, Heaven, and Earth. The Earth rotates around the sun. The moon rotates around the Earth. All in one direc-

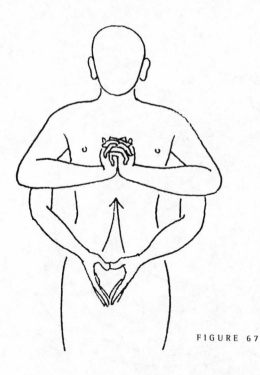

FIGURE 67

tion, this movement is a constant with its own inner balance. A tornado only turns in one direction and can only rise in one direction. Its external force is aggressive. Inside it is calm and controlled. At its center, all is perfectly still. Movement is Yang, calmness is Yin. Absolute peace is in the heart. Daytime is in motion. It is Yang. Night sleeps. It is Yin. After each hand posture's rotations, you bring your hands down and then switch the seal at the bottom of the stillness that lies at the balance point of Yin and Yang.

Just as you can read the life history of a tree in its rings, we too have rings that tell our story. Locating these rings, analyzing them, and healing them is a Taoist specialty. Master Du would heal his patients with this method more than with any acupressure point, for each person's rings are unique to him or her alone. Find your rings with the Yang and Yin rotations. Hear what they are telling you with the three hand seals. Become one with the messages of Heaven and Earth. Wrap yourself in the silk of the silkworm to bring positive change into your life.

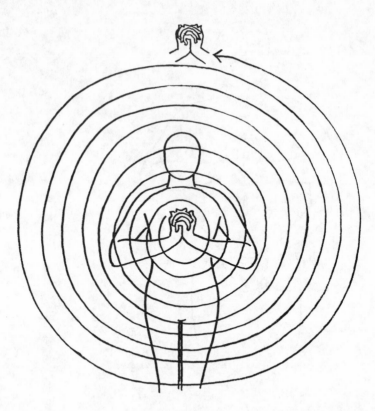

FIGURE 68

CLEANSING THE CRYSTAL

NOW THAT A sacred space has been spun, we come to the pivotal stage within the Healthy and Happy Practice of the 9 Palaces. Everything that has come before has been in preparation for this moment. The organs and senses have been opened, the circulation has been stimulated, the Qi has been energized, the mind has been calmed of all trouble and fear, and the Human, Heaven, and Earth realms have been unified into one field. Here the practitioner is able to reach into him- or herself at the deepest level possible. At this point, the body can be healed at the cellular level, cleansed to crystal clarity with purest Qi. This process is on one level executed with the mind

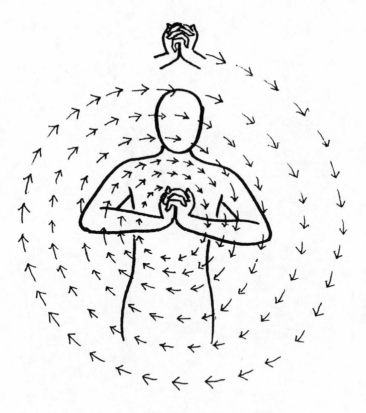

FIGURE 69

alone. However, you have guided your body into a special state where the mind is capable of affecting physical matter on a very subtle yet material level. These feats are a special training made possible by 9 Palaces Qi Gong. If you have practiced with concentration and emotional awareness until now, you will certainly feel its powerful effects.

To purify a crystal in the Taoist way, you must wash it in the ocean overnight, especially during the weeks approaching the Lunar Festival, then let it dry in the sun's rays. Like the crystal, we are going to let nature cleanse our organs. From the clasped-hands position that you ended your final hand seal with, the hands open and pull away slightly from the torso, the palms facing the body (Figure 70).

Without pause, return them to touch the body over the rib cage, plac-

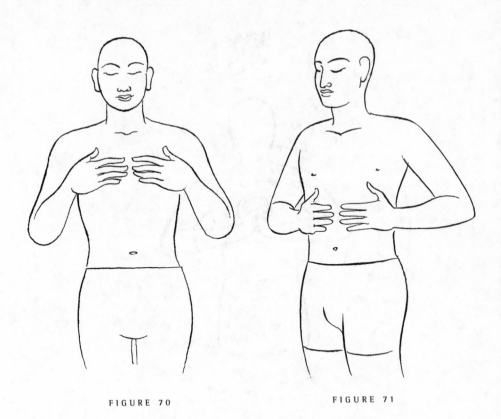

FIGURE 70   FIGURE 71

ing one palm directly over the spleen on the left and the other over the liver on the right (Figure 71). Gather up the energy of the liver and spleen into the hands, using the absorbing power of the *lao gong* points in the center of the palms to draw in as much of their Qi as you can. When you feel that you have firmly collected their energy, stiffen your fingers into rigid claws while still keeping the palms soft and cupped. These are the Dragon Claws. With their force, you are now able to remove your liver and spleen from inside your body. When you pull out the organs, the liver will bring the kidneys attached to it and the spleen will bring the stomach. Pull the organs out with your claws, keeping their Qi surrounded by the claws' might and held in your palms, tethered to the *lao gong* points. Pull them out and away from the body. (Figure 72.)

The sun rises in the east, which is the direction of the liver, and sets in the west, the direction of the spleen. When Dr. Wu treats a sick spleen, he

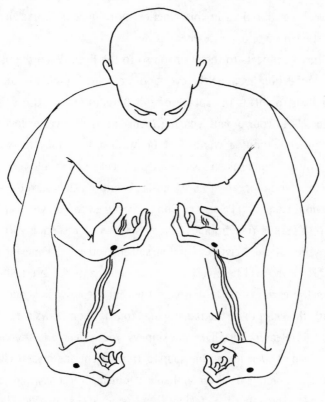

FIGURE 72

actually treats the liver to strengthen and replenish it. Cleansing the liver and spleen, we are moving from east to west, like the sun rising and setting in the heavens. Pull them out of your body with your Dragon Claws. Again, we are using the united forces of Human, Heaven, and Earth to attain our goal. The Dragon Claws activate the major meridians in the fingers. Be conscious of the Dragon Claws' strength. It belongs to the Human realm. It is the force of the Animal Spirit and the pre-Heaven soul, the prenatal potential. You must remove the liver and the spleen simultaneously. The liver's energy holds great waves of emotion. Its sensitivity and fluctuation mirror the shifting patterns of Heavenly Qi. Earth energy nurtures the spleen and the post-Heaven soul. The messages of Heaven are reflected in the eyes, related to the liver. You can sense the essence of the organs through the eyes. Dull eyes mean an ill patient. The heart has a mind that is grounded in the Earth forces of the spleen. We heal ourselves in this practice by using our heart's mind as a bridge between these opposite energies.

The heart connects to the eyes and so to the liver. When the palms are hot, the connection between the eyes and the heart is brought out. The *lao gong,* or heart point, is the source of this binding energy. Use your heart energy to talk to your organs, coaxing them out as the eyes of lovers speak to each other without a word. Your body must be totally relaxed while cleansing the liver and spleen. As you are practicing, you should feel as if you are swimming in an ocean of pure Qi. All of Nature's Qi is surrounding you. Each previous stage of 9 Palaces Qi Gong is designed to lead you step by step deep into this state. Your troubles have dissolved and wisdom is stirring. This is the rhythm of the newly integrated spleen. You have come far in your practice. Now you will be able to remove the organs. You are resting your organs in the currents of Qi, purifying them in their swelling tides, drying them with the warmth of the radiant sun. Your Dragon Claws are activated. Your heart is released. Your liver and kidneys, your spleen and stomach have been removed of their toxins and sparkle, transparent and crystal-clear.

Continue holding the liver and spleen outside the body, pulled as far away from the torso that they feel as if they want to snap back in. The spaces inside your body that you removed them from should feel hollow and empty. If you feel this sensation strongly, you know you have succeeded in bringing the organs out of your body. As you pull the liver and spleen out with the Dragon Claws, there will be a struggle as the ligaments that hold the organs in place will try to pull them back. Do not let go. This sensation may feel slippery or might fade in and out. If you need to, bring your claws closer to your body until the connection is again strongly felt. Maintain this posture until the energy link between the hollow places inside and the organs in your palms is stronger than the force trying to pull them back in. This link should feel stretchy and resilient, like a thick rubber band. If you don't feel it at first, keep your hands closer to your body and know that with practice, you will quickly strengthen yourself.

Something to remember is that this exercise is not a visualization. It is a physical experience that is guided by the mind and the heart. Know that the Qi will flow where your concentration and desire direct it. This is a simple sensation, easily felt if you have practiced each stage of the 9 Palaces up to this point with sincerity. Despite its simplicity, cleansing the organs is a profound manifestation of esoteric Qi Gong. As you arrive at this moment, you are tapping the true power of the 9 Palaces practice. Hold onto your organs, feeling them caressed and cleansed by the warm Qi of the sun. When your hands are very hot and you feel a cool or cold breeze blow through the empty spaces inside where your organs once were, you will know that you have completed your purification.

This entire process should take about two to three minutes. If at first you don't feel it, keep up your daily practice and eventually you will unblock everything you need in order to experience it fully. Slowly bring the Dragon Claws back to your torso, ending with the palms resting back over the liver and spleen. Gently pack your organs back into their proper spaces, pouring all the extra energy you have generated back into the body. As soon as you feel it suffuse you, with

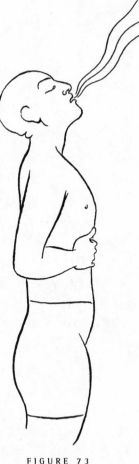

FIGURE 73

palms still over the liver and the spleen, tilt your head back and exhale all the air inside of your body in a long, slow stream to complete the detoxification (Figure 73). This releases all the toxic Qi from inside the body while leaving the beneficial Qi inside to rebalance it. On a physiological level, this exercise treats digestive problems and infections, cools the liver, and rids the organs of excess heat and toxins. Dr. Wu has also trained his patients who have serious immune deficiencies and cancers to do this practice daily along with their regular Western and Chinese medical treatments and has watched their conditions stabilize much more effectively.

Once you have returned the liver and spleen and breathed out the excess impurities, the next step is to use the hands to pull off and remove bad Qi from the liver and spleen, along with any other part of the body. In Taoist Qi

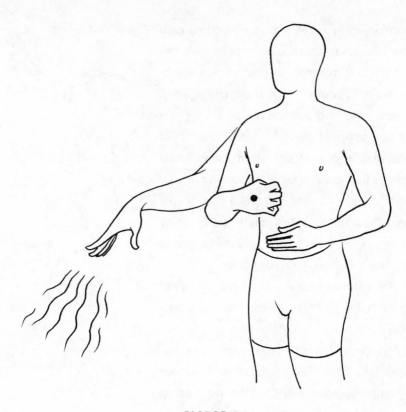

FIGURE 74

Gong healing, any parts of the body that are troubled or unwell are simply removed, the bad Qi tossed off, and nature is allowed to cleanse them. In out-of-the-way temples around China, some older masters may be seen performing strange manipulations on flowers. They are ridding the plants of bad Qi, helping them to grow strong and beautiful. A few days later, sickly plants that weren't growing are now in full bloom. Mind, heart, Qi, and action are perfectly combined, even in service of a small flower. First with the spleen and then with the liver, pull toxins and sickness out of the organs by letting the stagnation pool inside of the palm, using the *lao gong* points to draw out the pollution. As soon as it fills the palm, pull the hand away, throwing the bad Qi out and off the body in a quick whipping motion (Figure 74). Pull the toxins out of the spleen like this, tossing the bad Qi away nine times. Repeat nine times on the other side with the liver. Then continue anywhere in the body you have bad Qi.

If you have a shoulder pain, pull it off. If your mind is preoccupied, grab it and toss it out of your head. Pull sickness or pain out of any other organ or area of the body in the same way, using one hand for organs and muscles, whichever is convenient, and two hands together for clearing the three *dan*. Pull the sicknesses out until the area feels clear, light, and cool. Don't worry that your sick Qi tossed out of your body could accidentally land on someone else. You are using your mind to heal yourself on a very subtle and personal level. This is Qi Gong.

Years ago, when Dr. Wu worked in a large hospital in China, a mistake got made and the X-rays for two patients, one with cancer and one without, accidentally were switched. The cancer patient believed he was cured and his condition eventually was healed. The healthy patient thought he had cancer and wasted away, even though his doctors told him it was a mistake. This is how thoughts relate to cleansing the body and healing oneself. It is a deep connection that has to be recognized and respected for what it is. As you practice, you will discover this connection for yourself. Finish the cleansing by resting the palms momentarily back on the spleen and liver, then moving them out, away from the body, clasping them again and coming back to heart level, in the same posture you began with.

RELEASING THE HEART'S DESIRE

SETTLE YOURSELF WITH hands clasped at heart level. It is time for releasing the final thoughts, desires, and energies within the body before opening oneself fully to the power of the sun. You may feel perfectly calm and perfectly at ease physically by this point in your practice, and yet, there is always another layer that can be stripped away in the search for the ultimate emptiness. As we have illustrated many times throughout this book, *kong*, or emptiness, must come first in order to refill oneself with something new. However, there is no reason to deny yourself the deep-seated hopes and goals you might cherish in your life. Rather than turn your back on your human desires, the Taoists recognize that you will reach a richer sense of peace and tranquility if you can accept them, quickly come to a decision

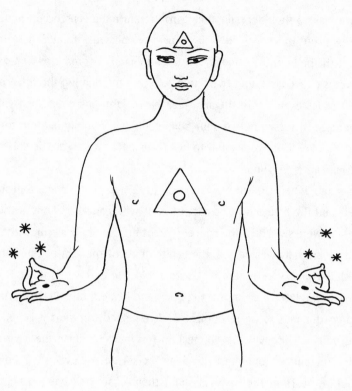

FIGURE 75

about the actions you are able to reasonably take and leave the rest to the ultimate will of the universe. If you ask the universe for help with sincere belief, it will come to you if your dream is for something you have even a chance of realizing.

While your hands are still clasped, focus your mouth and lips into your hands, to shield yourself from speaking words of harm, evil, and injustice. Focus your body into your hands to fulfill the will of the Tao. Focus your mind and heart into your hands for constant positive thoughts.

The hands open up from their clasped position, palms up, fingers forward at spleen and liver level, the thumb and forefinger of the left hand forming a circle. The right palm is kept flat and open (Figure 75). As you spread your arms, place all your hopes, dreams, and plans into your palms. Be sincere within your heart and it will work. Be kind to your parents while they are still alive. Don't wait until they are dead and your love and kindness are meaningless. The forefinger and thumb together form a mudra of working for positive outcome in your present life. We are not guaranteed reincarnation with consciousness and free will after we pass from this plane. It's a question of cause and result. We reap what we sow. We might see bad people eating well, in spite of their selfishness and cruelty, but we are not in a position to see every side of their existence. A good heart helps to relieve sin, for this life and for the next life to come.

Although in this practice we use the mudra of thumb and forefinger together, to cultivate this life, it helps to put our place in the journey into perspective by thinking for a moment about another similar mudra. The thumb and pinkie together with the hands in the same posture is for the final cultivation, to become an infinitesimal particle, without rebirth, without diminution, just a speck of dust in the infinite universe.

After you feel your palms become heavy with all your highest aspirations, in a sweeping motion, cross your arms over your body, palms facing to the back, lowering yourself down a bit by bending the knees in toward each other in a half-squat (Figure 76). At the same time, say out loud "HA!" in a forceful, breathy, and short exclamation. Feel like you have let all the air out of your lungs and your chest has sunk in slightly. From this position, the arms flip back over, palms up. In the same fluid motion, pull the arms, palms up, elbows bent, back in toward the body while bending the knees further and pronouncing a breathy and audible "HO!" (Figure 77). This "HO" is short and explosive, more breath than word, the lips rounded and the mouth loosely rounded. Feel as if you have released even more air from inside. Do not inhale yet, as there is going to be one final sound. Settle yourself for a brief moment, then continue.

Slowly straighten up while the hands come up to form a slightly rounded shape, like the symbol of Taiji. The palms are facing each other and the fingers are somewhat rigid, their energy expressed. Focus the Qi between the palms until they reach heart level, then push out from the body until the arms are almost completely extended (Figure 78). During this movement, which should be done slowly, let all the remaining breath in the body come up from the diaphragm and out of the mouth in a controlled stream while saying "HUUUU." Push all the way out to a tree in the medium to far distance

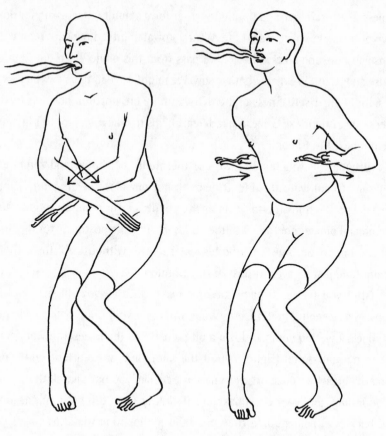

FIGURE 76   FIGURE 77

that you feel an affinity for. Take this literally. Practicing outside is not an absolute must, if the other option is not practicing at all. However, this tree will ground you and will become your partner in this practice over time, if you return regularly to your same spot. Even if you practice indoors, if you see a tree outside the window that you feel a connection with, use it as your focus. As you push out, your hands come together further, and your arms raise very slightly in the process, the hands now taking the shape of the triangular solar pyramid.

Each of us has a magnetic field. When practicing with more than one person, the healing increases. Practice around trees. Spend time around children. Old trees will give you inspiration. Young trees have plenty of extra

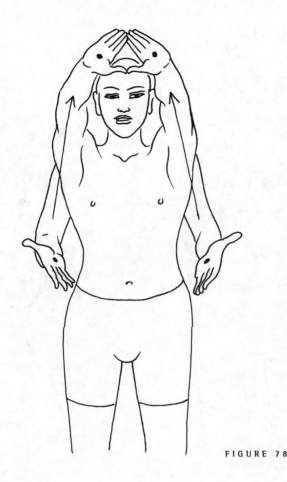

FIGURE 78

energy. You may even look like a tree. Dr. Wu was a problem child. When seeing his master always spending time climbing trees and being close to them,
he asked, "Why don't you get married? Do you like those trees more than
women?" Master Du didn't care very much for this insolent remark. However,
there is much beautiful Qi to be gathered by communicating with nature.
Heaven, nature, and humans are all related. The sounds *HA, HO,* and *HU* and
the motions are as one.

After pushing out, the hands, which have come together to form a triangle between thumbs and forefingers, now open out again in a rounded arc,
arms opening out and around until the forearms are slightly higher than parallel with the ground (Figure 79). Finish this motion by pressing the finger-

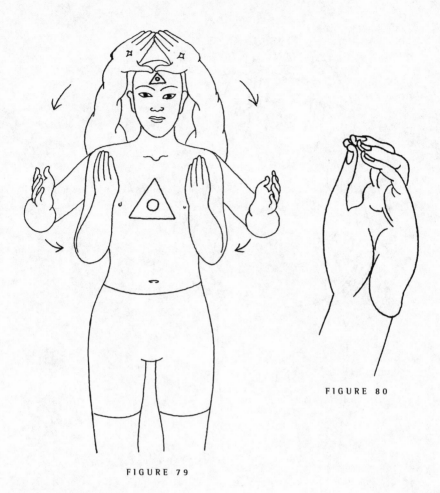

FIGURE 80

FIGURE 79

tips together, all touching the thumb in a pointed shape. This mudra is known as the Five Finger Mountain (Figure 80).

As you feel the thumb making contact with all the fingertips, silently invoke the colors of the Five Elements one by one, in the order of the fingers: green for the thumb, red for the forefinger, yellow for the middle finger, white for the ring finger, and black for the pinkie. See the colors green, red, yellow, white, and black, in that order. Think each color one by one in sequence. Look at the colors. Feel them permeate your consciousness. It's very important to surround oneself with the colors.

In Beijing, there is a special spot where five colors of earth are combined in the soil. Standing in the Five Finger Mountain posture while contemplating each color, we are creating a similar place of power for our practice. Our bodies take the shape of the pyramid as we invoke each color. Each color is governed by a Lord; each organ has its own mind, consciousness, or deity. Announcing each color within ourselves, we are calling down these deities. Standing firm in this calm and solid stance, we are taking on their five consciousnesses as our own, assuming the role of the Five Elements.

Mountains represent the patient or student. Water equals prosperity and a successful career. Forests speed advancement. Qi Gong gathers Qi from all three of these environments. With this posture, you are turning your body into a landscape such as this. At this time, you can let your heart relive any emotion or experience from the past. This posture is excellent for getting in touch with old matters and memories from this life, or lives previously lived. Five Finger Mountain will help fortune and spirit guides to come to you. As you stand visualizing the colors of the five Elements surrounding you, allow toxins and unresolved memories to be released. They will arise as a thin trail of "smoke" from the fingertips (Figure 81). From within this deep state of union with the Five Elements, they will flow effortlessly from you, without any special attention.

After a few minutes standing with the Five Finger Mountain mudra, the hands move into a palms-up fist, with the thumb bent inward and the rest of the fingers resting along its top edge, forearms parallel with the ground. Pay special attention that the tip of the middle finger presses onto the first joint of the thumb (Figure 82). Keeping the hands in position, chin tucked in, pivot 180 degrees on the left leg until facing in the opposite direction (Figure 83). Keep the leg you are pivoting on solid as possible, and land firmly as you finish your turn. You don't need to turn quickly, just with precision and stability. At this point, you should be deep within a sense of clarity and calm, so this should not be very difficult to accomplish.

We are at last prepared to gently absorb the healing Qi of the sun into our bodies. The crystal has been cleansed, and now it is time to charge it with power. As soon as you have pivoted around, stretch your neck out and down, chin to the chest, exposing the back of the neck to the sun. Take in the Qi of

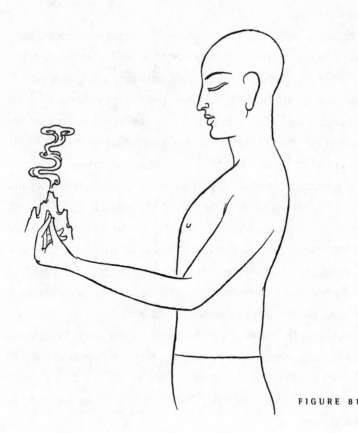

FIGURE 81

the sun (or simply universal Qi) through the point at the center of the highest bone on the ridge of the spine (Figure 84). All the purification, all the emptying, all the mental and physical effort have led to this. You are a perfect vessel ready to receive the sun into yourself. Continue absorbing the Qi until you feel it shoot from the neck to the shoulders and from there to the brain (Figure 85). This should take approximately thirty seconds to one minute. Again, the 9 Palaces is meant to energize the body, so proceeding at a steady pace without losing yourself in the middle of any one particular movement will bring maximum force to your practice. Heaven is giving back to you now what you had lost before. Let it come to you quickly, in a burst of energy and awareness.

After you feel the sun's fire filling these points, straighten your neck and pivot again on the left leg until back in the original position (Figure 86).

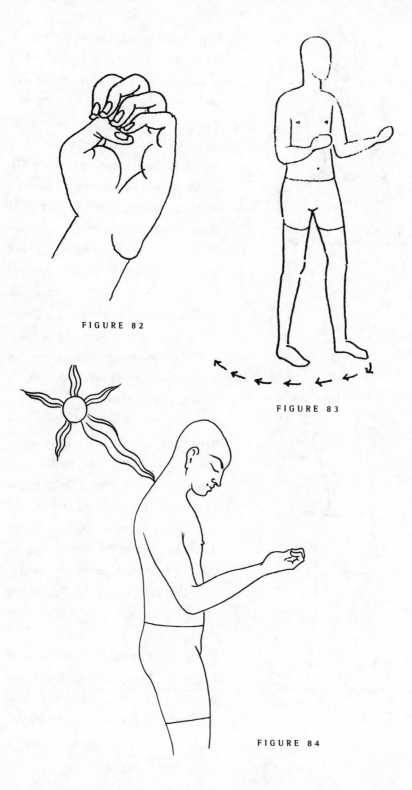

FIGURE 82

FIGURE 83

FIGURE 84

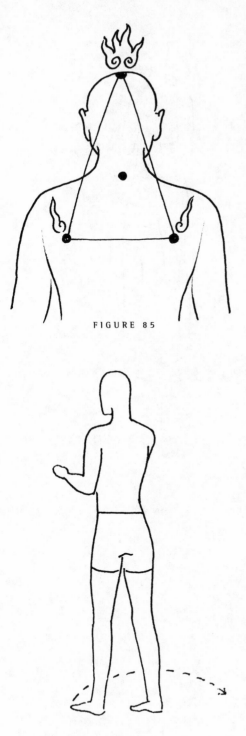

FIGURE 85

FIGURE 86

When pivoting, never move the left leg. Try to keep it as stable and firmly rooted as possible. Tilt your head all the way back, exposing the throat to the sun. Absorb Qi through the point at the center of the throat opposite the point just used at the back of the neck (Figure 87). Commune with and receive the sun into yourself. Continue absorbing Qi until it flows from the throat all the way down to the lower *dan tian* and shoots back up and out again. This hollow pathway starting from the throat point is the road along which we communicate with the universe. Again, spend thirty seconds to one minute. The universe is ready for you; it only takes a moment to make contact.

After the sensation of exchange has passed, straighten the head again. With fingers still in same fistlike position, bring the right hand up to lightly touch the left shoulder, turning the fist over in the process. Continuing the movement, extend the arm up and out forward from the head, gently opening the hand, palm facing out. Repeat this salute to the sun with the left arm (Figure 88).

Now that the arms are outstretched up forward from the head, gently flow into the next motion. Allow the hands to effortlessly describe a small rounded circle and as if this circle has become a

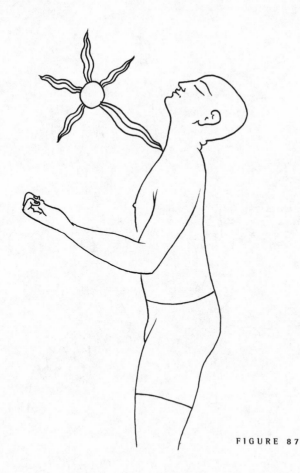

FIGURE 87

ball of energy, lift the cupped hands holding it up over the head, as if presenting a consecrated vessel to the sun. Allow energy from the sun to flow
into your palms.

With both arms extended toward the sun, cupped hands feeling the Qi
streaming in, announce: "I am the son/daughter of the sun. I am receiving
Your unlimited power. Help me to overcome all difficulties and obstacles,"
You can say this aloud or silently to yourself, but either way, bring a feeling
of sincerity, gratitude, and confidence to this statement. It is interesting to
note that you come to the sun not as a supplicant making obeisance to a god,
but as a child venerating the parent who has given him or her life. You are
at once paying tribute to the source of your sustenance and proclaiming as
your birthright its infinite energy.

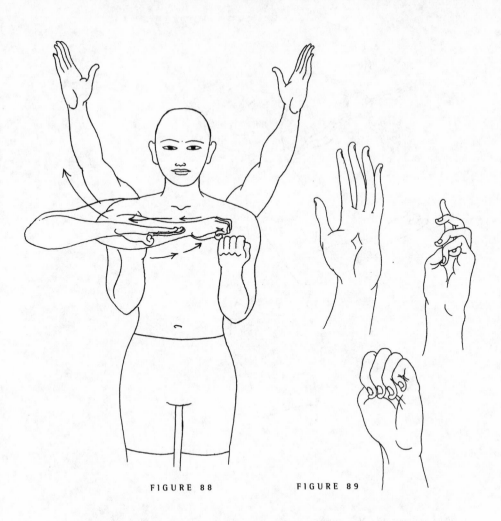

FIGURE 88   FIGURE 89

Slightly separate your cupped hands, allowing them to open naturally. Press the thumbs into the center of the palms, then, one by one, cover the thumb with the fingers, starting with the forefinger, ending in a fist (Figure 89). We are preparing for the ultimate absorption and release of solar and universal Qi.

Clench your teeth solidly, tighten the anus up toward the body, and dig the toes of both feet firmly into the ground. Pull down the arms, with the fists facing the body, while bending at the knees, chin tucked in. While you use muscular force to tighten the body into this squat, use your mind to direct and concentrate all your Qi plus the Qi that you have collected into the lower *dan tian* (Figure 90).

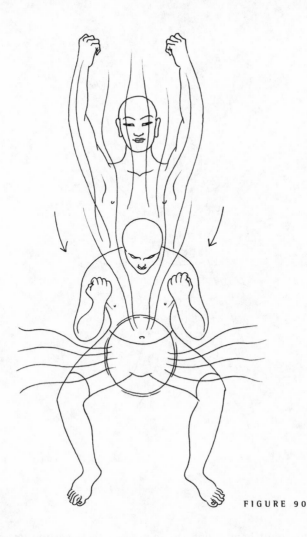

FIGURE 90

Rotate your fists at the wrist to face outward, then immediately thrust your arms and whole body upward, hands opening, arms coming back up and out, releasing the Qi with a large "HA!" (Figure 91). Expel the breath inside of you with this sound and feel all the power you have accumulated bursting outward through every pore. The anus, which was clenched when you pulled in, unlocks, allowing even more energy to shoot up through the center of the body. Hold your arms up and out, fingers forward, until new sensations arrive in the fingertips. As in the symbol of the 9 Palaces, you have used the Five Elements and each of the organs, from liver to heart, to burst through joyfully to your Original Self.

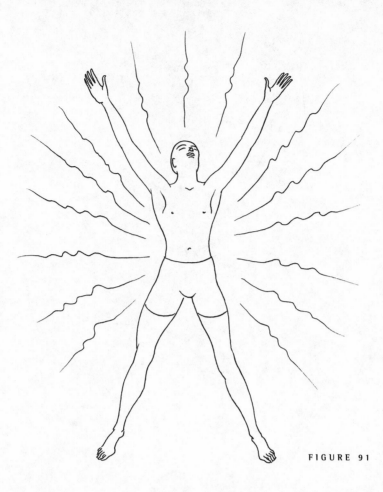

FIGURE 91

With the right hand, bring the arm down to touch the left shoulder, hand open, palm down. Draw the hand to the right shoulder across the collarbone, then run your palm down the right side of the chest, lightly touching the body at all times to end in a half-triangle at the lower *dan tian*, the thumb at the navel. Repeat with the left hand, completing the triangle at the lower *dan tian*, thumbs meeting in the navel. You have closed the salute and formed a square, solid seal on your body to collect the energy you have just bathed in (Figure 92).

With hands in a triangle on the lower *dan tian*, gently bring the left leg together with the right, bend the knees slightly and bow your head (Figure 93). This closing posture allows all the Qi generated to settle easily within the

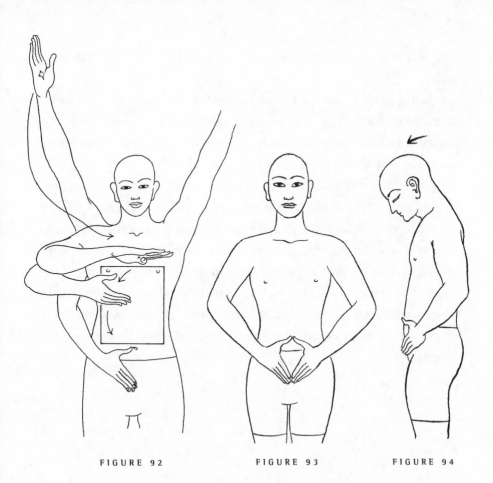

FIGURE 92   FIGURE 93   FIGURE 94

body, as well as giving a moment for contemplation (Figure 94). Feel the Qi rising up from the lower *dan tian* into the heart. After a small pause, straighten up and store all the accumulated Qi in the lower *dan tian*.

Drop your hands, step out, and quickly return your consciousness to a normal state of awareness. Snapping out of the deep meditation of the form quickly helps ground your new energy. As a student and patient of Dr. Wu, I would often be surprised at how, after a very deep treatment, he would clap his hands and have me practically jump off the treatment table. Over time, it became apparent that this was the best possible training for teaching the body to absorb large quantities of Qi without feeling sleepy or spaced-out afterward. You will use your newfound force most efficiently and for greatest vitality if you can quickly return to a relaxed but present sense of self after your practice. Direct yourself with your mind, and your body will follow.

You have now completed the 9 Palaces Solar Qi Gong, as it has been practiced for generations. Just as you have opened yourself outward to unite as one voice with Heaven and Earth, you have joined the ranks of students and scholars who have sought knowledge and insight from within.

The 9 Palaces Qi Gong is a symphony of breath and light, of sensation and emotion. It is organized with intelligence, like the movements of a cosmic concerto. It leads you step by step on a profound journey, and yet at the same time you are the conductor. You decide the tone with which it is played, deep in the core of the body's microcosm or expanding out to the macrocosm of the universe. Experience its various moods. Use your heart and mind to interpret its sweeping grandeur and its quiet reveries, its silences and its thunder. With practice, you touch the largest and smallest reaches of the infinite.

NINE

The Butterfly Emerges

AS A YOUNG man, Confucius traveled from afar to ask Lao Zi a question.

Instead of answering, the great sage took three steps forward, paused to

gave his petitioner a penetrating look, then took three steps back and sat

down. After this, his audience was over and Confucius was sent on his way.

Only after walking along the verdant mountain trail for some time did the

meaning of this teaching finally dawn on him. He had come all this way to find an answer to his blazing dilemma, but he needn't have made the exertion. Instead of a journey of hundreds of miles, to make his decision, all he needed were three steps forward and three steps back. It was the perfect balance of *wei* and *wu wei*, action and nonaction. A perilous journey could have been avoided, if he had only known to take three steps forward to examine his situation closely, then three steps back from it to give himself the space for an objective overview. Next time you have an important decision to make, try this exercise. Stand up and literally walk forward three steps. Look close. Then take three steps back, letting go of your opinions with each step. When you are walking backward, your mind doesn't have the time to concentrate solely on the chronic internal monologue. Your body has to pay attention to the simple act of walking. When you are done, you will have balanced yourself well enough for the moment to find a clear-headed solution to your problem. This is classic Taoist behavior. By combining the mental, emotional, and physical in one easy and elegant gesture, you change your attachments and opinions. Always seek the broad perspective. Choose your actions quickly and decisively. When you have more objectivity, you will have fewer problems as well. If you don't wish too high, you won't fall too far.

After reading through this book, you might still be asking yourself, Why practice Qi Gong? After all of this information and this long list of exercises, what am I really accomplishing? If taking three steps forward and three steps back were all it took to clear the mind and gain a higher perspective, then what is the purpose of all this complexity? Very often in the West, there is a certain dichotomy between the effort that is taken to reach a new understanding and the quality of that understanding. Revelation, flashes of insight, sudden states of nirvana that come in a pure, all-consuming leap of consciousness are judged more authentic, as they come seemingly untouched by the struggles of the ego. Somehow, achieving a clear, empty lucidity seems antithetical to any force used to achieve it. How is spending an hour every day going through the various operations of 9 Palaces Qi Gong any better than the labors of a medieval alchemist toiling in his laboratory? The Taoist recognizes that while a sudden realization can be most easily reached through simplicity, retaining that awareness and moving forward in one's life with it is another matter entirely.

It's quite common for people to experience intense sensations of heat, vibration, or lightness during their Qi Gong practice; see flashes of light, color, geometric patterns, or visual imagery; or even hear sounds or voices. However, these experiences are not necessarily proof that you are practicing effectively. For example, one student told Dr. Wu that during the eye/liver exercise she would often see many colors all at once, even though she was trying to see only green. Dr. Wu's answer to her was to remember that the body is a chemical factory. Keep the mind clear when releasing toxins. Different-colored Qi comes out with different moods. White is happiness, related to the heart. Purple is fear, related to the kidneys. Muddy, indeterminate colors relate to an angry liver. The Taoists call the world of emotions the "Colorful World." When you see a lot of colors as you practice, you are a very emotional person, or perhaps simply too smart for your own good for dwelling on the colors instead of on the purpose of your meditation. In the eye/liver practice, green protects the eyes and shrinks the liver back to its original size. Whoever succeeds in seeing green while practicing this exercise accomplishes this due to his or her sincerity, concentration, and attunement to the body's cues, not due to intellect or "smarts."

Conversely, some people might say, "When I meditate, I tune out everything. I'm not involved with this 'colorful world.' My mind is a blank slate. I'm into myself, very calm and held in." Dr. Wu would say in that case, you might as well take your clothes off, go to bed, and have a nice nap instead. You will certainly be calm and quiet when you are fast asleep. To make progress in your training, there are always definite mental processes you need to perform as you meditate. When you meditate, your brain must work with your body as an active partner. You cannot simply zone off, tune out, or go to sleep. As you look back through the 9 Palaces practice, you will see that even during the most basic standing posture, you are always bringing a mental image or directed emotional state into play. This will positively augment the quality of your practice and aid your cultivation.

In fact, *cultivation* is the key word here. What the Taoists realized about spiritual work was that even while you must journey deep beyond your mind and emotions to experience a heightened perception of the world outside, this "colorful world" was not an end in itself. You have to work consistently

with the fabric of the mind and emotions to refine it, in order to elevate it to a state of genuine communication with the universe. Practicing Qi Gong is like building a pyramid from the base up. With each day's practice you are laying the building blocks so that when you get to that point where stillness and clarity occur, your enlightenment is total, permanent, continuous. Enlightenment is no mere philosophical metaphor. The Dragon Gate Classic texts relate how a full year's daily practice of the 9 Palaces will reveal the complete meaning of the *I Ching* to the sincere student. Many of Dr. Wu's students have experienced a heightened, visceral awareness of the interplay of Yin and Yang energy in their daily environment, an understanding of how these combinations produce the stuff of reality and the clear light of the universe that lies behind their permutations. Make no mistake about it: Qi Gong leads to a new way of seeing, a new life to lead.

REN YI TIAN DI

SO WHAT, THEN, is Qi Gong? Is Qi Gong a religion? A philosophy? A physical workout? A mental exercise? An occult ritual? In fact, Qi Gong is any and all of these. Our lives stand in the midst of the Three Generations—past, present and future—and the Six Relationships. Be happy with what you have; it's all precious. We practice Qi Gong to bring up our level so we can more fully appreciate what we have in life and the nature of life itself. Eyes, nose, ears, urethra, anus, and mouth: these nine openings correspond to the Nine Stars in the sky. We come from the heavens. Within the particle, the cosmic seed of the universe, there is no birth, no death. The Milky Way is the silver river that carries us through.

Lao Zi is the originator of 9 Palaces Qi Gong. He taught the 9 Palaces before he composed the *Tao Te Ching*. In fact, Li Er was his actual, given name. Lao Zi is a respectful term for "old person." *Lao* means "old" and *zi* is an honorific participle, a symbol of rank. Of the numbers one through nine, nine is the highest and the largest. It has *zi*. *Zi* is a concept that encompasses a great deal. You must be a master to have Zi added to the end of your name. "Tian Zi" is the Heavenly Master, or Emperor. A beggar is "Jia Hua Zi." It's the same for a beggar and an emperor. He Sha is a monk and Huan Sha is an emperor or president. Gan Sha is a beggar begging for food. Each of these three lives have the same ending to their names and lives' work. Are their fates so different? There is a cosmic rotation we are all a part of. In Tibet, in each family, one son traditionally must become a monk, dedicating his life to spiritual cultivation in order to help the family. The emperor's cultivation lies in the dedication and service he undertakes for the people. The beggar's cultivation develops forgetting about everything, renouncing material needs that hold many others down. All these destinies follow the path of cultivation. An emperor of the Ming dynasty was advised to become a beggar, to heal the wounds his rulership has created. He came out from the palace with a golden bowl, going from door to door begging his bread, visiting a hundred families from all levels of society. His Taoist advisors passed their insight into the equality of all people to their king and countrymen alike with this act of cultivation. We are all equal in the opportunities for cultivation we can find in our lives.

This equivalence is fundamental to Lao Zi's 9 Palaces theory. Even within a grain of sand, the whole world exists. Yin and Yang are just the back and front of the sun. The human and the universal are one, unlimited, infinite. As a part of this infinite array, there is equally no limit to one's own potential when the true self is known. Work hard and go higher and higher. You don't have to look far to see examples of people pushing themselves or being pushed beyond their limits, succeeding at feats no one thought they could ever accomplish. You must believe. Heaven and human united can be found fitted within a grain of sand, or expanded to fill the immeasurable space of the universe. During practice, release yourself and let go, then come back into your innermost core. Push away as far as you can. Take your sickness and trou-

bles outside your body, then return within, cleansed and revitalized with universal energy. As small as a grain of sand. As big as the infinite.

Why 9 Palaces Qi Gong? Human and Earth are one. The *I Ching* says that wind, heat, dampness, dryness, and fire are all illnesses based on external, seasonal origins. As the seasons fluctuate, so do each person's health and fortunes respond. Human and Heaven are one. The Taoists believe the number of stars in the sky and the number of people who have ever lived are one and the same. Every person has his or her own personal star in the heavens. Birth is the Big Dipper, and death is the Small Dipper. Half your soul is here, the other half is in the sky as a star. Life travels from East to West, finding treasure and opportunity along the way. Your being is intimately connected to this totality.

The 9 Palaces Qi Gong helps you to link to your other half and by extension, to the rest of the cosmos it is part of. Our consciousness travels a path much greater than the years we spend here on Earth. Many aspects of your future path are predetermined in the heavens. We each have a pre-Heaven destination. Finding it is the cosmic mission of your soul. Life is neverending. The symbol for the motion brought forth from the birth of the universe is the right-facing swastika. Lao-Zi said everything follows this curve, this generative energy. Zhang San Feng, the originator of Tai Chi, embraced this same theory as its foundation. All the galaxies and everything contained inside them travel on this shared clockwise course. Within the breaths of *"HA," "HO,"* and *"HU,"* you discover this primordial rhythm within your own body. After death, we travel through the Six Realms to arrive at our life's location in the karmic sequence. By raising your awareness, making the effort to expand your connection to the planet, bringing harmony and communication into your life with your cultivation, you are healing your past, enhancing your present, and readying yourself to play your role in this grand scheme.

Deities are always being approached by people who request protection. The fact is, you must give first. The Buddha won't help unless you serve first. Practice Qi Gong, ethical living, and good deeds, pray, read sutras, and spread the word. Then God will help. It's like swimming. If you want to move forward, you must first paddle. A man came to Dr. Wu and said he has worshiped Buddha for thirty years and has received nothing—no guidance, no fortune, no enlightenment. Dr. Wu said, "This is because you have done nothing for the Buddha." All the blessings of Heaven are waiting for you, waiting for you to reach forth to become a part of its hosts.

By practicing Qi Gong, you help others. Trees produce oxygen. The Taoists see the human body also as a tree. Just as a tree gives off oxygen to benefit the environment, we help others with our light—the spiritual light of the Yuan Ying, the inner light of your original self. As the relic of the Buddha's finger lit a darkened crypt with its spiritual radiance, your 9 Palaces practice trains your light to come forth, emanating a field of calm and harmony that touches all you encounter. You must first balance yourself by practicing. This is no small task. The 9 Palaces will guide you in the right direction, each day's practice another stepping-stone toward reawakening your original wholeness. There is no limit to the level of truth and oneness you can find within yourself, no final ceiling to your cultivation.

Qi Gong lies in a realm beyond simple worship or prayer. It is direct communication with the universe. Once you are living as one with your true self, you will reach others. Continue to practice Qi Gong. On the wheel of all creation the beginning point is also its endpoint: tree, human, and dragon. When you have opened your Ming Men point, you will release yourself up into the universe and be able to help. No longer merely a Human Tree, you have become the Dragon Tree. Male and female combined, Human and Universe combined, the righteous energy of your spirit is set free. No matter

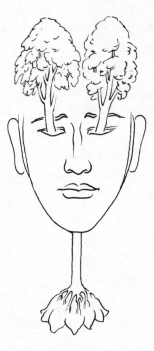

how alone in the world you might feel, you are merging the best of yourself with everything around you. You might not ever know who you are helping. When you see a person, animal, or plant you are fond of, this feeling is the human and universe combined. A cultivated practitioner can even relieve dead souls of their struggles and entrapments with his or her love. This devotion is called the Mercy of the Heart. This is mercy from heaven. What some might think of as God's love, we each have inside our being, waiting for release and expression. Every fruit bears a seed to continue itself, to give birth to a new tree. This is also the Qi Gong way—the path of the Human and Dragon Tree. Practice mercy and ethics to replant your soul, to reseed the world with the love within your heart.

I AM THE LORD OF MY LIFE

ACCORDING TO THE *I Ching*, humans and the universe coexist together as one. However, blindly accepting this as fact is no different than accepting any other type of dogma. Unquestioning faith of an obscure, intellectual philosophy was never the intention of the original Taoist masters. Taoist Qi Gong holds a unique place in the history of religious and mystical thought in its insistence upon achieving a physical awareness of truths such as the oneness of all things. When you practice Qi Gong, it's helping you to commune with the universe, to feel with your heart and sense with your body what nature is trying to tell you. With your 9 Palaces training, you are creating a personal relationship with the universe. The salient point to remember is that as you practice, you are developing your natural ability to talk and communicate with the world around you.

The fact that this communication operates on the most simple and pragmatic physical level is part of the profound power of Qi Gong. The *I Ching* teaches us that as humans, we succeed or fail as we are willing to adapt to nature's cues. This is not a question of belief. For the most basic survival, we need to physically adapt to spring, summer, fall, and winter. If it's freezing outside, aren't you going to put on warmer clothes? If the crops are not planted at the right time of year, people will go hungry. Your ventures will have greater success if you time them according to seasonal demand and supply. A doctor will be wise to stock up on cold remedies before flu season is in full swing. A fisherman will make sure his boat is in order before the lake thaws.

Qi Gong takes this awareness to the next level. You may be going with the flow in your life, but as new situations arise, how do you respond to them? How do you recognize the opportunities that lie within the changes as they come? How do you sense their arrival with enough time to set a new course? There is information trying to come to you from all around. Do you know how to see these signposts as they appear? Even as the ancients codi- fied the teachings of the *I Ching* to aid in this knowledge, ultimately they knew that it is our own sensation of and personal response to the universe that is the ultimate determining factor in making the best choices for our lives. Lao Zi's ultimate message within the *Tao Te Ching* is, "I am the lord of my life, It's not up to the heavens to decide." I am my own lord right here where I stand. I decide my own destiny right now as I take action: a very fine wording of a wise philosophy for us all.

We have to practice Qi Gong so that we can change our own fate, change our own life. Qi Gong forms a powerful bridge between heightened self-awareness and fuller understanding of the forces at work upon one's life. There is a traditional Chinese saying: "At age thirty, we first stand up on our own two feet. At forty, one learns to listen to one's own counsel, no longer influenced by outside opinion. At fifty, we finally begin to understand what our true purpose in this life is." Qi Gong practice speeds up this development, aiding you to cut through the obstacles that stand in the way of self- knowledge and growth. Use Qi Gong to gain mastery over your life. As your understanding of the workings of your body and mind and your responsive- ness to the messages found around you in the outside world increase, you can be assured that you will have many opportunities to do good for yourself and all those around you. They will come naturally to you as you protect and improve the natural harmony between your inner self and the outer world. You will be in an ideal position to understand and benefit from the messages that nature generously brings to us all.

Serious Qi Gong practice will change you. It will change your outlook on life. There's no set result, however. As you bring your own personal feelings and perspectives to your practice, you will benefit in your own individual way. It is self-regulating, bringing you the particular balance and harmony that you need. You learn how to read the messages in the world around you that are meant just for you and how to trust the truth of your inner voice when it speaks to you. Talking with students of 9 Palaces Qi Gong over the years, I found it interesting to note how wide a range of varied yet interrelated, positive results can occur, even in people with widely differing backgrounds and experiences. Besides improvements in their health, many reported new ways of seeing people and events and some had unusual events happen that could not be simply explained.

> "My outlook on life has changed, gravitating toward things that I'll benefit from to improve my health and keep my body energized and clean—including people, food, environments, just a natural gravitation. It's almost like the body continues to reach a cleaner state of health and naturally starts to point north—like a compass."

> "I don't do any fast-moving rigorous exercises anymore, yet if I wanted to run five miles I know I could. My lung capacity and muscle endurance is more than equipped to handle the challenges. I'm able to walk long distances without fatigue. I guess the odd thing is that it happens subconsciously. If you only stick to a physical regimen, it's always a challenge. Your body feels the pain, but the truth is by practicing Qi Gong and getting Qi and oxygen into special places in the body that are opened by the movements, I've become lighter and buoyant, needing less muscular strength, at the same time preserving my physical

body. For my age, I thought I was in pretty good shape, but my body was polluted. Years of smoking, drinking—you don't realize how far you have floated away from truly being healthy until you start back."

"Dr. Wu can tell the issues the students in his classes have and he incorporates it into his lesson. So when he mentioned how the ear-flicking balances your blood pressure, I felt like he was thinking of me. Before learning 9 Palaces, I was on Chinese herbs for my high blood pressure, but he taught that if you flick your ears at least nine times in the morning or any time this would also balance the blood pressure. So I tried it and it really works. I noticed my blood pressure drop within thirty minutes. My pressure had been up because of problems at work, but I find that 9 Palaces Qi Gong is more beneficial even than the Chinese herbs. I feel wonderful. I'm very active and my blood pressure is under control. If it hadn't been for Qi Gong and Chinese herbal medicine, I would have had to be on Western drugs for the rest of my life."

"I'm more flexible, more energetic. I'm not a young person, but if you put me next to a teenager or a young person, I'm not bragging, but I can walk as fast as that teenager. I work for a very busy office and you have to run around for nine hours a day. The Qi Gong gives me that energy to get me through the day. Some young people in the office have a hard time keeping up with me."

"Internally, you become very sensitive and are able to feel what your body really wants and what it doesn't want. When something as simple as drinking a soda gives you a warning, it's pretty interesting. Your body definitely senses it, wants to reject it. Sometimes I drink mineral water and my body starts to tingle. I can feel it running into my veins and through my blood. My brain feels like it can receive the signals of what's good and not good for me."

"Qi Gong enables me to know what's going on with the environment and people. It can be something as simple as being able to pick up on somebody's feelings, which you might not usually notice, if they're hiding it. On an internal level, you might see them in a dream and it will reveal exactly what they need, or need you to do to rebalance them."

"One night I was driving home from work about 1:00 A.M. As I was driving, in my mind's eye, I saw a car accident. I continued to drive for approximately another mile and as I entered the freeway on ramp, all the traffic was backed up and there was an accident on the freeway. It happens when it needs to. It's not necessarily everything that's going on—just things that you could make a difference with will be revealed.

Many times when these things are revealed, all it takes is a simple phone call and you can make a difference in someone's life by understanding someone's situation from an introspective perspective. Just as you can help someone else, practicing Qi Gong helps open up the channels in order to receive your own guidance and help from spiritual guides and family members."

"I had a new boss choose me to be her new employee. When I was in the office about a month and a half after being employed by her, a voice told me she's going to get another secretary. I didn't believe it. But it was without fail, she got a promotion and she couldn't rest until she told me that she was hiring a new secretary for herself. It warned me about a month and a half before. Sometimes I've had warnings two and three months ahead."

"One day I was practicing and I saw my classmate walk across the grass, like a flash in my third eye, but there was no way that he could have been in that place at that time."

"The very first class I ever took with Dr. Wu, he taught us this one exercise to do at dawn, as a greeting to the new day. I got up at dawn and did it and went back to sleep. Later that morning, as I was talking on the phone, I looked over at this vase of completely dead, dried-up cut flowers that I just had been lazy and hadn't thrown out and they were all back in bloom! I remember getting off the phone and walking around the vase being amazed, but I was very young at the time and just sort of shrugged it off, thinking, 'It must just be the good Qi.' I'm not sure that something like that could ever happen to me again, but it really showed me the power of Qi and I've been a serious student ever since."

Qi Gong is what you make of it. It is a personal tool for your own individual self-discovery. If you are not inclined to approach your practice from a religious or mystical bent, you are not somehow disrespecting its power. This is what Lao Zi was trying to get across by stating that each person is the architect of his or her fate. It's for you to decide how you would like to make Qi Gong a part of your life. It is not inherently negative or less noble to practice strictly for health or good fortune. The fact is, if you practice Qi Gong, over time you will dramatically reduce your chances of getting sick. Sickness won't come to you, because when you practice Qi Gong, you strengthen the vulnerabilities of your body. The sick Qi is blocked from coming to you. Misfortune will not come to you because you have strengthened the vulnerabilities of your mind. The bad-luck Qi will not come to you. They can't get near you. Who is to judge that by taking steps to safeguard your health and mental well-being, you have not done enough for the world? Who's to say that creating a solid foundation of health and happiness won't make you a more effective person in all areas of your life? Only you can decide. "I am the lord of my life," Based on this fact, Lao Zi developed the original 9 Palaces

Microcosmic Orbit practice to proclaim and enhance this awareness within ourselves. The messages of Heaven are there for you to read.

Beyond material sustenance, there is another, deeper impulse, yearning for fulfillment, that resides within each living being. Especially as the modern world has created so many new challenges and dislocations to overcome, we labor to hold on to our individuality, our desire to make a difference. In simpler times, it was easier to know what our roles were and what contribution we could make to our society and our belief system. Now we struggle to make a meaningful mark on our world at every turn. This isn't simply a question of egotism or the desire for power and fame. As sentient beings, each of us has a profound urge to create, to give forth, to sing of what lies inside like a bird on the wing. This is the life force. Its strength wells forth from deep within. We might call it creativity, intelligence, spirituality, wisdom. It is unique to each individual. There are countless ways to present one's special gift to the world. One person might be a dancer, an artist, a lover, a philanthropist, a healer, a mystic, a parent, a teacher. The story of the self lies dormant in no one. Whatever expression you use, know that you are giving voice to something meaningful within you that also holds great meaning for the greater good.

Our individuality is our glorification of the diversity of life. Our personal communication with the universe is a holy offering to this multiplicity. As lord of your own life, you are not only preserving your original abilities, you are naturally extending a great gift to the rest of humanity and to the source of all creation. Make no mistake about it: the search for self-knowledge is a spiritual search. It stems from the desire to share, to contribute, to communicate more effectively with the world. The Taoists understood that authenticity and personal integrity are paramount to becoming a truly realized human being, and that a realized human has the greatest ability to foster positive change in the universe.

Never fear that your opportunity to express the spiritual urge inside you has been blocked, polluted, lost touch with. Qi Gong will nourish you. Your cultivation will bring the spiritual energy from within yourself into everything you do. What is the true nature of Qi Gong? What is its true purpose? Here, finally, is our answer. Qi Gong is personal expression. Use Qi Gong to find your inner voice. Let your 9 Palaces practice be your song, your dance, your prayer. When you complete the many stages of 9 Palaces Qi Gong, you have used every nerve, muscle, and organ in your body in service to your health and well-being, as well as the health and well-being of the universe. Your practice is your message of love to the universe. Your training is your path toward ever-new levels of personal, creative, and spiritual expression. Step by step, exercise by exercise, you have put your feet to this road, as a pilgrim, as a seeker of your own truth. Let each day's Qi Gong be a magnificent performance. However you define an exquisite act of beauty and power, give your practice life as its truest manifestation.

Practice with your heart, practice with your feeling, practice with your deepest sincerity. As every fiber of your being strives to become one with all, lift up every emotion to join your body in this union. Revel in your perfection, for it will be a beacon of light for all those who come in contact with it, an inspiration for all those just starting on their own journeys, a joyous pillar of strength for you and your loved ones. As Zhuang Zi's butterfly at last bursts free of its chrysalis to float effortlessly upon the currents of Qi, may the blessings of 9 Palaces Qi Gong unite you with the Tao.

INDEX

health, benefits of Qi Gong to, 22–23, 127
Healthy and Happy Practice, 28–31
   warmup, 28–29, 124
hearing
   animal's, sensitivity of, 57
   improving, 58–59, 150–52
   of internal body sounds, 150
   loss of, 58
   sending it far, 151
heart
   communicating with the kidneys, 93–94
   connection with the eyes, 184
   exercises for, 153–60
   as red, 130
   as true ruler of body, 66, 79, 156
Heart channel, 42
heart problems, 60, 82, 123
heart rate, 46
Heaven and Human United as One, 133
helping others, 154–55, 209–10
hepatitis, 21, 129
high heels, wearing, 66–67
hong hua (transubstantiation), 11
hopes and goals, accepting them, 187–89
hormonal balance, 38, 104
horses, 124
Hsin I Chuan, 37
Hua Tuo, 122
Human Tree, 209
hun (spirit soul), 47, 86

I

I Ching, 26, 37, 65, 172, 206, 210–11
illness
   causes of, 21, 146
   food better than herbs, 137
   locating and assessing, 83

immune system, 23–24, 38, 185
impossible experiences, 14, 61, 128, 212
impotence, 118
individual practice, 3, 16
individuality, each person's urge to develop, 216–17
indoors, practicing, 32–34
injuries, 91
insomnia, 60, 68
intestines, connection with anus, 21
isometric exercises of Qi Gong, 127

J

Jin Jing Yu Yeon (Refining the Golden Jade Elixir), 159–60
jing (our essence)
   nourishing through meditation, 42
   postnatal, 96
   prenatal, 94
   seated in Ming Men, 94
joints
   pain in, 48
   storage of Qi in, 103–4
journal, keeping a, 33

K

kidney disease, 93
kidneys
   as black, 130
   communicating with the heart, 93–94
   connection with ears, 21, 47–48, 57–58, 150, 151–52
   and inhaling, 147–49
   and long life in men, 150
   and pre-Heavenly foundation, 114
   regulating, by working on the ears, 153

Yin and Yang (*continued*)
 circuit of energy between, 111–12,
  178–79
 coexistence of, 22, 78
Yin channels, 26–27
 location of, 114
Yin energy
 related to absence of sun,
  26–27
 See also Yin and Yang
ying (baby), 86
yu ji (point on hand), 116
yuan (source or spring), 86
yuan qi (Original Qi), 38

Yuan Ying (Immortal Fetus), 86–88
 born in *dan tien*, 117
 growth of, 87–88, 95
 helping others with the light of our,
  209–10
 released into the universe, 95–96,
  121

Z

Zhang San Feng, 208
Zhen Guo Fashi Da, 60–61
Zhongnan Mountain, 2, 172
Zhuang Zi, 2, 3
zi (master), 207